Durham Coal
A People's History

Edited by

Andrew Clark & George Nairn

A coal train from Silksworth Colliery to South Dock, Sunderland, against a backcloth of snow-covered Tunstall Hills.

Previous page: A group of men at Easington.

Copyright © Andrew Clark & George Nairn 2001

First published in 2001 by

The People's History Ltd
Suite 1
Byron House
Seaham Grange Business Park
Seaham
Co. Durham
SR7 0PY

ISBN 1 902527 82 8

Contents

Introduction   5

1.   A County Built On Coal   7

2.   Railways   75

3.   Wartime   89

4.   The Price Of Coal   95

5.   Looking After One Another   111

6.   The Big Meeting   127

7.   At Play   147

8.   Pit Life   161

Acknowledgements   174

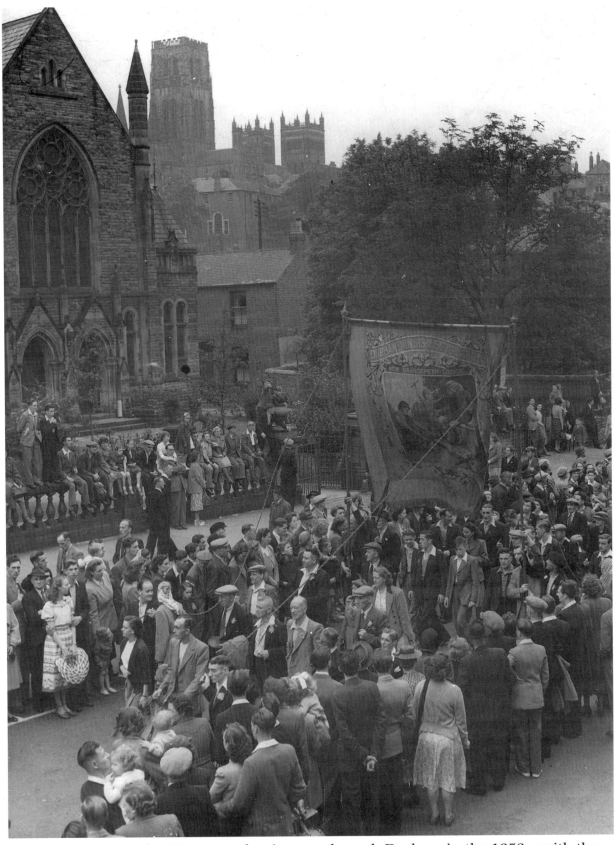

New Brancepeth Lodge Banner makes its way through Durham in the 1950s, with the Cathedral in the background.

This rare view of Andrews Houses Colliery is from around 1905. The pit was owned by John Bowes and Partners and was located just south of Marley Hill Colliery. Andrews Houses Station is now part of the preserved Tanfield Railway.

Introduction

This collection of photographs and stories is not intended to be a definitive history of coal mining in County Durham. Instead it is hoped that, through many unique images and first hand accounts, it will provide a glimpse of an industry that once dominated the North East. Today there is little remaining to show that Durham was once a county built on coal but there are many who have vivid memories of the effect it had on the area.

We start this People's History with a tour of the county as defined by its old borders – so we have included Sunderland, Gateshead and South Tyneside. Here we see views of many of the pits in the area. Some are well known while others have almost been forgotten. The men, women and boys who worked in the industry are also featured and several tell their own stories – some with humour and others with sadness. Other aspects of the coal industry are also shown, including the railways, coke works, office work and some of the other trades associated with mining. We also feature the Durham Miners' Hall the home of the DMA and the NUM who have campaigned and fought to improve the life of everyone connected with the industry.

The 'Dark Days' of mining are recalled with stories of wartime as well as injuries and disasters in the pits. The price of coal was a high one and every pit in Durham has its share of tragic tales. In this book we feature the disasters at Brancepeth 'A' Pit; Wingate Grange; the Burns Pit, West Stanley; Glebe Colliery, Washington; and Easington. Sadly, however, there are many other stories of loss of life in the collieries. The hard times of stoppages and strikes are also illustrated with photographs of soup kitchens and people scavenging for coal.

Adventure Colliery, West Rainton, was formerly owned by the Marquis of Londonderry. It was reopened by the Rainton Colliery Company and this postcard shows new buildings being erected in 1914. It was well known for its very good household coal and would be supplied to all NCB officials.

Working in such a dangerous job created a sense of comradeship between the workers who believed in taking care of their marras. In the section, 'Looking After One Another', we feature some of the schemes and organisations that aimed to improve the lives of pitmen and their families.

Although times were often hard in the coalfields, the miners knew how to enjoy themselves. There was no bigger day than the Durham Miners' Gala and there are many memorable images and poignant memories of the 'Big Meeting'. The pitmen's pastimes – football, cricket, bowls, leek growing, pigeon racing, whippets and music – are shown in the section, 'At Play'.

Finally, we look at pit life as a reminder of days long gone. From coal deliveries to washing day, we show the everyday events in the colliery village.

The authors owe a great deal to all those who have been kind enough to share their memories and photographs of coal mining in Durham. They have shown enormous generosity towards us. A generosity which is typical of the people of the mining communities of County Durham.

Andrew Clark
George Nairn

SECTION ONE

A COUNTY BUILT ON COAL

Two examples of famous Durham architecture – a colliery pithead and Penshaw Monument. The Monument was built for the first Earl of Durham, John George Lambton, whose family were one of the major land owners and coal owners in the county. The pithead is that of Herrington Colliery. Like many former colliery sites the land has now be reclaimed and landscaped. There are now only a few reminders of the industry left in the county.

Wet And Dry Water
by Arthur Curtis

My father was a miner. Fifty years ago he mined for coal under the North Sea. His job was extremely dangerous, and every day as he left, he and Mum would have a hug and kiss because they both knew that this might be their last meeting. 'Canny on,' she'd say, and he would walk the four miles to work in the pit. He hated every minute of it. His body was pock-marked with purple scars where he had injured himself and coal dust had got into the open wounds.

He hated it so much that he wanted us boys to choose any work but that of pitman. He talked to us often of the dangers, but he knew that words were not enough, so each of us, when we were eleven, were taken for a day's shift at the pit face.

My day arrived. I didn't know whether to be excited or horrified. Horrified, because I just knew that this was to be the day when the wooden pit props would creak noisily (a warning to all pitmen to move out – fast). Excited, because today I would see the 'dry water' he talked about, and the rats that ran over him as he knelt or lay down to use his pick to dig out the coal.

When we arrived at the pit, he changed into shorts, boots, and knee pads before collecting for both of us a Davy safety lamp and helmet. We then entered a cage with space for about twelve people. There was no talk. I stood in this silence knowing why it was so. I, too, was scared speechless.

The cage hung on a very thick steel cable, and when the door was closed, the brake on the cable was released. We didn't simply descend, as you do in a lift; we dropped in free-fall as bungy jumpers do. My stomach seemed to bounce off the inside of my skull as we plummeted. And, like a bungy jumper's rope, as the brake was applied, the cable stretched then contracted and our cage shot up, down, up, down, till we slowly settled to a final descent to the earth beneath the earth. We were now a kilometre inside the earth's crust. We walked out of the cage, and I silently congratulated myself on having

A hewer at work in a pit before the Second World War. Note the flat shovel used to load the coals into his tub.

A miner pushes his full tub of coal at a Lambton, Hetton & Joicey Colliery in the 1920s.

not cried out, vomited, or clutched at Dad. Electric lights lit the surprisingly large landing area where men and coal were lifted out of the pit.

We moved on to a series of flat-bed carriages pulled by a tiny engine, and travelled out under the North Sea, till Dad told me we were over three miles from the coast. Nagging doubts filled my mind: about the ability of a row of fifteen-centimetre-wide tree trunks to support the ever-creaking roof. The roof above which lay a kilometre of sea. (Who checked these pit props? How often? Was it good quality wood? Were Dad and his friends deaf, or what? I could hear quite clearly the message of the props: 'Get out! We are about to crack! Can you swim? Upwards? For a kilometre? Through a stone roof?')

The electric lights disappeared behind us, and our safety lamps gave only flickering, frightening impressions. The walls and ceilings of rock grew ever closer to each other, and to me. The engine stopped. The rails beyond that point were narrower. We slipped off the carriages and I joined Dad, taking his hand to let him know I was all right – but I know he knew the real reason for holding hands, and he never told anybody.

Our lights seemed brighter somehow, but perhaps it was the smaller space they were required to light. The passage was narrower, and so low that the men had to bend. The light of the lamps reflected in the water we trudged through.

'Dry water,' said Dad.

My feet were wet. What did he mean? Was this some sort of joke to play on newcomers?

The men gradually moved off down different passages until Dad, his partner, and I were alone. The roof was so low that even I had to bend as we slopped further forward in the 'dry' water. My lamp now picked up a movement of something bigger that a rat.

'Dad?'

'Don't fret, lad; it's our pit pony. It pulls wagons of coal back to the engine; that's what the narrow tracks are for.'

The pony was a tiny creature that just fitted into the height of the tunnel. It responded so happily to my pat that I decided to hug its neck tightly. (It told no one the real reason, either.)

Here was the coal face I had heard so much about. While the pony and I consoled each other, I was able to move my lamp around and catch the reflection in the eyes of the rats. I now understood why Dad's bait was always sealed in a tight tin canister.

'I'm a hewer,' Dad said. 'I dig the coal out of this wall with my pick, while Jimmy here shovels it on the wagons. The pony pulls them to the train, then brings empty wagons back to us.' I crouched there, hugging a pony and watching as Dad knelt to his job. His knee pads settled on the rough rocks and he swung his pick into a wall of gleaming coal, grunting with each swing.

We were all sweating now – for different reasons – and the coal dust was streaked black on our bodies. No pits, and few homes, had showers. I knew that Dad – we – would return home in the evening and bathe in front of the fire in a small tub, half filled with cold water, and warmed by boiling water from kettles from the open fire.

I looked forward to that as I listened to the wooden ceiling supports twinging and twanging under the pressure of rock and water above us. The sounds became a sort of music to me, music with words: 'Look at those rats, there are no cats, and I'm gonna fall right down on you.' Neither of the men seemed concerned, so I just clung to the pony's neck and left it to them to decide when to run. I was ready, though.

Bait time. Tight canisters and water bottles opened; sitting in wet 'dry' water. The conditions were enough to tell me that I didn't really want to be a miner, but the final decider was when Dad took all three safety lamps and covered them with Jimmy's shirt. (He couldn't turn them off because you needed a match to relight them – and that would be a fatal mistake in a gas-filled pit.)

To say it was dark is an understatement. It was an impossible blackness in which you immediately lost any sense of direction. There was no sight; only sound: the rats squishing and squeaking; the pit props singing and signalling; the pony snorting coal dust from its nostrils; and we three panting and drawing the same, killing dust into our lungs.

'Dad?'

'Yes son?'

I tried to sound casual. 'What's wet water?'

He unwrapped the shirt holding the lamps, and I saw his white teeth against his coal-black face. 'It's here now, lad. Dry water's what you walk in. It's already there, and you don't get paid extra for working in that. But you get a bit extra for working in wet water. That's what's dripping from the roof. It's fresh from the North Sea a few metres above you.'

He held his head up to the dripping roof, and rubbed. His face reappeared, but eye sockets, neck, and body were still covered in coal dust as he turned to me.

'D'you want to be a pitman, son?'

'No thanks, Dad.'

He collected his pick, half-knelt and half-lay on the rough-hewn rocks, and went back to work. As I held the pony's neck I could see beyond the rats to a smile that almost lit the pitface.

His work was done. His job went on.

Pit pony and putter underground at a Lambton Collieries pit, around 1905.

Two images showing the cramped underground working conditions.

Douglas Pocock in his book, *A Mining World – The Story of Bear Park*, described life down the pit before the Second World War:

'It was a noisy world, with shuddering windy-picks (if not hand picking), shot firing and rock falls, besides the general shovelling and moving of coal. In quieter moments, besides listening to the rocks answering back (the roof groaning or cracking), attention might be drawn to the squeaking of mice in the cavities, thereby realerting the pitman to the safety of his bait in his jacket pocket. With sandwiches as likely wrapped in paper as in a tin, care always had to be exercised over the hanging of the coat. (It was not unknown for mice to be shaken out of a pocket after returning home.) It was the bottle of water rather than the bait, however, that was the pitman's best friend, since, without proper ventilation, the work was hot as well as arduous and was often tackled stripped to the waist. The air could also be foul since there were neither toilet facilities nor road sweepers in the underworld.

Danger was ever present. While fatalities averaged one a year and serious injuries were almost commonplace, the tell-tale mark of the active pitman was what he called 'buttons' – scabs on the vertebrae, periodically renewed as the bent back was again tortured by rocks or supports of the low, rough roof. On top of all these was the possible cumulative effect of coal dust and flickering oil lamp on lung and eye respectively, so that towards the end of the pitman's battle with coal he should be defeated by pneumocniosis (or other chronic respiratory diseases) or by nystagmus.'

Gradually, conditions in the Durham Coalfield began to improve and new technology radically changed the working lives of pitmen. However, there were always dangers associated with mining. Here are three more modern underground scenes.

A Huwood Slicer Loader in the Maudlin Seam, Washington 'F' Pit. It was the oldest working colliery in the country when it closed in June 1968. Part of the colliery was preserved and opened as a museum in 1976.

Horden East Shaft, December 1973.

Two miners on top and bottom man riding belts around 1980.

Like Father Like Son
by Dennis Fisher

This is a photograph of my dad, Jack Fisher, taken in July 1963 when our mining days ended with the closure of the seam where we both worked through threat of flooding at Chilton Colliery. The

pit lasted a bit longer by working the Hutton seam before it closed for ever in 1966.

The photograph was taken at the top of our garden in the mining community village of Auckland Park. Note the old gas lamp and the coal house let-hole where many a load of coal was shovelled up into it.

Just for the record, as both Dad and myself were coal hewers, the price we were paid then was one shilling and eleven old pence a ton. You needed about five ton a shift to make some sort of decent living. All the coal hewed was by windy pick and without the pit pony we'd never have made a penny. I wonder how much a hundred weight of coal is bringing today?

The flag Dad is holding is the very first NCB one that Chilton Colliery ever flew off its pithead mast on reaching its weekly production target after Nationalisation, 1st January 1947.

An early view of Chilton Colliery.

Brancepeth 'A' & 'B'

A postcard of Oakenshaw Colliery sent in 1906. Known as the the Brancepeth 'B' Pit, it was sunk in 1855 by Straker & Love. In the mid 1930s the company employed over 2,000 at Brancepeth 'A', 'B', 'C' and Drift, Brandon Pit House, Brandon and Willington.

A group of men take a break from working on the cages at Brancepeth Colliery 'B' Pit in February 1916.

A group of trainees and instructors at Brancepeth Colliery 'A' Pit in Willington in the late 1940s. The electric shop is on the left and coal cutting repair shop on the right.

Lost Childhood

George Parkinson, the son of a miner, was born at New Lambton in 1828. He followed his father down the pit when he was a boy but left mining to become a well-known Methodist Preacher. In 1912 he recorded his life as a preacher and a miner in the book, *True Stories of Durham Pit-Life*. Here he describes the time when young boys worked in the mines:

'The miners' lot at that period included very long hours of labour, with very short hours for rest. No standard of age was then fixed for boys entering the pit, but they were sent to work as early as six or seven years of age; not as is sometimes alleged, from mere heartlessness on the part of the parents, but under pressure of growing family needs, which was very keenly felt in my early years, owing to the long-continued low rate of wages and the high price of provisions. Nor was any legal time-limit fixed for their dark and dreary toil, so that, irrespective of age or circumstance, boys were generally called from bed at three o'clock in the morning. Meeting at the pit mouth at four, they descended into the regions of darkness, where for thirteen or fourteen hours a day – and often for more – they abode in gloom, made visible by the feeble flickering light of a small tallow candle, or the still feeble reflection of the wire-shaded Davy lamp.'

Boys ready for work at a Durham pit. Some of the lads look very young. This was perhaps, for some of them, their first day of employment. A lifetime down the pit is ahead of them. How many of these boys finished school on a Friday and started at the pit the following Monday. No doubt joining their fathers and brothers at the only employer in the area. Note the lad second from the right has the typical miner's pose – holding his lamp with his thumbs in his belt.

A booklet of 'Special Rules' from the Coal Mines' Regulations Act, 1887, described the regulations for employing 'boys, girls and women'.

'Boy' means a male under the age of 16.
'Girl' means a female under the age of 16.
'Woman' means a female of the age of 16 or upwards.
A 'Week' begins at midnight on Saturday and ends at midnight on the succeeding Saturday.
A 'Period of Employment below ground' begins at the time of leaving the surface and ends at the time of returning to the surface.
If the age of a boy or girl is misrepresented by a parent or guardian, the parent or guardian, and not the owner, agent, manager or employer, is liable to a penalty.
A register of particulars concerning boys, girls, and women employed has to be kept.

Below ground:

Girls and women of any age Boys under 13	May not be employed or be for the purpose of employment.
Boys over 13	Not for more than 54 hours in one week. Not for more than 10 hours in one day. Eight hours must elapse between the period of employment on Friday and that on Saturday, and 12 hours between other periods of employment.

The immediate employer of every boy, if he is other than the owner, agent, or manager of the mine, shall, before he causes the boy to be below ground, report to the manager, or to some person appointed by the manager, that he is about to employ the boy in the mine.

Above ground:

Girls under 12 Boys under 12	May not be employed.
Girls under 13 Boys under 13	Not for more than six days in one week. Not for more than six hours in any day if employed for more than three days in a week. Not for more than 10 hours in any day if employed for only three days or less than three days a week.
Boys of 13 and upwards Girls of 13 and upwards Women	Not more than 54 hours in one week. Not for more than 10 hours in one day.
Boys Girls Women	Not to be employed between 9 pm and 5 am. Not on Sunday. Not after 2 pm on Saturday (except in those mines in Ireland which may have been exempted). Eight hours must elapse between termination of employment on Friday and the commencement of employment on Saturday, and 12 hours between any other two days. Not to be employed continuously for more than 5 hours without an interval of at least half an hour for a meal. Not to be employed continuously for more than 8 hours without an interval or intervals for meals amounting to not less than an hour and a half. Not to be employed in moving railway wagons.

Murton

Murton Colliery, 16th August 1907. Murton Pit was known for its distinctive head gear which was a German Koeppe Winder.

New Pit Head, Murton Colliery.   7218

A Monarch Series postcard showing the New Pithead at Murton Colliery. A dark day in the history of the pit was in 1942 when 13 men were killed after an explosion. The colliery closed in 1991.

A group photograph of Murton Colliery Officials gathered together to celebrate the Record Daily Drawing, 4249 tons, on 1st April 1909.

Looking for coal at Murton during a stoppage.

Pit Ponies
by Derek Gillum

Pit ponies played a major role in the Durham Coalfield. In 1937 there were more than 13,500 ponies working in the North East and more than 10,000 of them were in Durham. In the 1870s Lord Londonderry established a stud farm at Seaham. Later many ponies were bought from William and Fred Laws of Willington. They traded with the NCB and private coal owners from 1915 to 1964.

There were many famous ponies in the Durham Coalfield, such as 'Lion' from Harraton Colliery who won numerous prizes at shows all over the country. Regular pit pony races were held at Bowburn and many other colliery villages with proceeds going towards charities such as the Durham County Hospital.

Training pit ponies at Tribley Pit, Hett Hills, around 1903. On the left is Mr Widderfield and on the right is William Rule. Ponies were trained on the surface of the pits where they were led around a dark circuit while pulling tubs.

Pit pony, training at Harton Colliery, 25th March 1912. Popular names for ponies included: Tot, Peter, Fet, Bob, Bill and Dobin.

A pony and tub from Newton Cap Colliery. This is a postcard sent from Bishop Auckland on 25th July 1907 to Battersea Park in London. The message reads: 'One of the features of procession we had on Saturday last, pony and tub of coals. Hoping you are keeping well.'

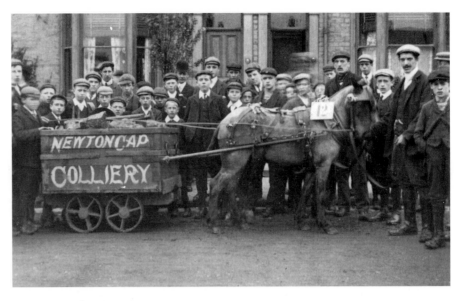

Mr Dixon and Golightly with a pony at Hedley Pit. The writing on the tub says: 'Plenty coal for the man who burst the pipe.'

Ponies and their drivers coming to bank at South Pelaw Colliery. The last ponies to come out of a Durham pit were at Sacriston Colliery when it closed in 1985.

Thrislington

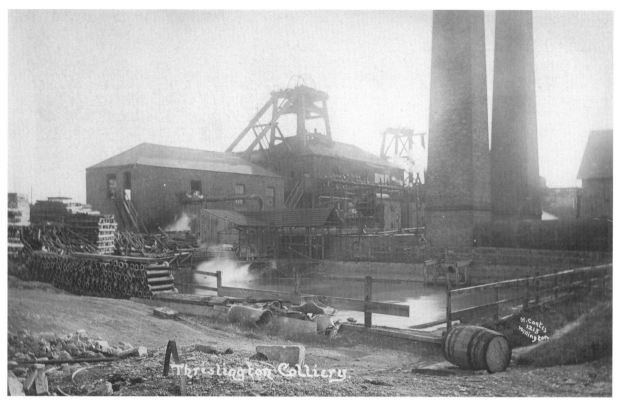

A postcard of Thrislington Colliery before a devastating fire. A message on the back of the card reads: 'I send you this PC of Thrislington pit. You perhaps know it took fire in the engine house on Nov 25th and the heap-stead was totally destroyed but fortunately the shaft was not much damaged, and they expect to get started work again in a few weeks time. It has made a dull Xmas here but some men got started at Mainsforth.'

Thrislington Colliery after the fire on 26th November 1911. Before the Second World War, Thrislington was owned by Stobart & Co Ltd who also ran the Fishburn Colliery. In the mid 1930s over 1,200 were employed at Thrislington Pit. The colliery ceased production in 1967.

Wheatley Hill

Wheatley Hill Colliery (No 2 Pit). No 2 Pit closed in 1968, the No 1 Pit had closed three years earlier.

Wheatley Hill Colliery Band, 1910.

Hard Times

Peter A. White in his book, *Portrait Of County Durham* (published in 1967), gives a forthright view of the miner's life:

From the pitmen's point of view coal is the dirtiest four-letter word in the language. Coal has exploited him, sweated him, underpaid him, swindled him, ruined his health and maimed him. In many cases it has even buried him. Its centuries old story in Durham has been a tale of the pitman's running battle for social justice ... he is justified in his attitude, for the history of Durham coal is a long chronicle of human greed and man's inhumanity.

Iron harnesses discovered at Wearmouth were worn by children dragging coal-laden tubs along narrow underground roadways. Illustrations of those grim days did something to awaken the nation to the horrors of the pitman's life when the Royal Commission made its report about a century ago. But conditions did not improve overnight. Durham was the last place where the yearly bond survived, a practice which bound the pitman to his coal owner in something like medieval serfdom. And wily coal owners were not slow to take advantage of his ignorance, slipping in a penal clause, reading the new bond very quickly, and offering a guinea to the first man to 'make his mark'. Small wonder that Lord Londonderry, creator of Seaham Harbour, spoke so powerfully in the House of Lords against the raising of the school leaving age a century ago. But did anyone really believe his plea that, 'a boy of twelve should be learning his trade not wasting his time in reading and writing?'

Some of the 93 Boldon Colliery putters who appeared at South Shields County Court to answer breach of contract summonses in the 1920s. At this time there was a lot of unrest at the pit. In 1929 over 600 Boldon miners were fined 10 shillings each for laying the pit idle. The stoppage was caused after forty-three hewers were not paid the minimum wage.

Miners' soup kitchen at Waldridge, 5th May 1921. The *Daily Herald's* 'Save This Miner's Child' was a popular slogan at the time.

Men and boys at Waldridge take a break from scavenging for coal to pose for the photographer during the 1926 Strike.

Aerial Ropeway

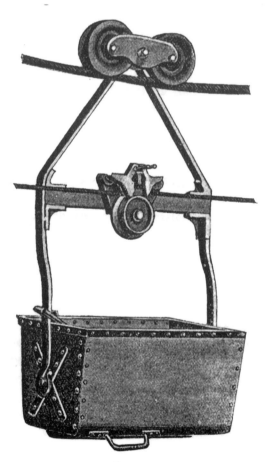

One of the ropeway's tubs and its 'attachments'.

The aerial railway which transported coal between Esh Hill Top and Malton. The system was known as the 'Otto' Ropeway and was a German design. When it began in November 1900 it was one of only a handful in this country.

The ropeway was two miles long with supports every 100 yards. Each tub carried five hundredweight of coals and took seventeen minutes to travel the two miles. When it was first opened, three hundred loaded tubs could be transported each day.

Esh Hill Top Colliery was worked for Usher College with coals going to them for domestic use. The aerial ropeway was built after the pit was sub-leased to Colonel Sadler MP who was the proprietor of Malton Colliery. Transportation difficulties from Esh Hill Top were solved by linking the two pits by the ropeway. Malton was served by rail.

When Colonel Sadler took up the twenty year lease, it was estimated that there were nearly a million tons of coal to be mined.

Malton Colliery was finally closed in 1961.

Locos

The loco 'Charlaw' being delivered to Sacriston Colliery in 1912. This saddle tank was built by Peckett and Sons of Bristol. It was transferred to NCB No 5 Area on Vesting Day and was scrapped in 1962.

Workmen with a steam locomotive and coke wagons at Hamsteels Colliery. This 0-4-0 saddle tank, 'Hamsteels No 3', was a 2ft 10in narrow gauge loco built in 1877 by Black Hawthorn of Gateshead. Hamsteels Colliery, near Quebec, was opened in 1867. The colliery closed in 1924 but was reopened in 1932, with an aerial ropeway to Malton Colliery.

Pithead Baths

Wearmouth Colliery Pithead Baths. The baths were opened in February 1931 and originally could accommodate 2,016 men with 48 bath-cubicles. Not long after it was opened the bath was extended with a further 28 cubicles to help accommodate a total of 2,692. Including this extension, the total cost of the baths was £26,838.

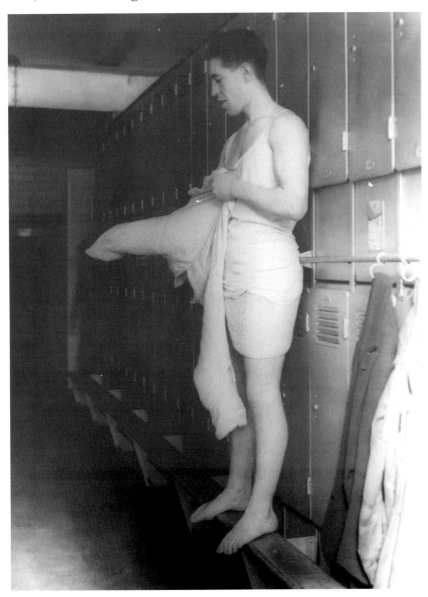

A miner at Silksworth Colliery Baths, 1937.

J.N. Pace in his book *Ryhope And Silksworth* recalls the time before pithead baths: 'Men went home wet and blackened with coal dust. They bathed in a tin bath in front of the fire. Clothes had to be shaken and beaten clean out of doors, usually by the girls of the family, while boots were thoroughly dubbined to make them waterproof. Before the advent of pithead baths, many of the older generation of miners *never* had their backs washed, maintaining that this weakened them! Instead they had them dry-scrubbed with a piece of 'harn' (sacking).'

The Bather's Handbook of 1956 gave these instructions for using newly-opened pithead baths at Handen Hold Colliery:

'First day – Going to work – On the day that the baths are first put into use go to work in your pit clothes. Take your clean clothes with your soap and towel with you in a parcel.

Go in at the 'clean' entrance. There you will be given, in exchange for the bather's registration slip, a key and a card with the number of your two lockers.

Go to the clean clothes locker room and find the locker bearing the same number as your key. Hang your clean clothes and hat or cap on the fittings provided. Your boots or shoes should be placed in your locker in the insulated containers provided.

You should hang you overcoat in your locker on the hanger provided. Then lock up, withdrawing the key carefully and go to your pit clothes locker – which has the same number – and put your soap and towel in it. Lock it up and go on to the pit entrance. There you can grease your boots and fill your water can.

First day – Returning from work – After shift on the first day go in at the pit entrance.

Clean your boots under the revolving brushes before entering the pit clothes locker room. When you have undressed and hung your pit clothes and safety helmet in your pit locker, take your soap-tray, soap and towel, lock up, and go to the bath house.

The showers have been adjusted to give the best spread of water, so all you have to do is to turn them on. DO NOT interfere with the nozzles in any way, they are easily damaged.

It is a good idea to finish off with a cold shower to avoid catching a chill. Try to keep bits of soap off the floor in the cubicle; they are dangerous to other bathers.

Take you towel, soap and soap dish to your clean clothes locker and leave them there for your next shift.

After the First Day – From then onwards you go to work in clean clothes, hang them up in your clean locker, take your soap, soap dish and towel, lock up and go to your pit clothes locker to dress for work, leaving soap dish, soap and towel ready there for your return.

A boot-brushing machine from the 1930s.

Boot-greasing apparatus.

Hetton Lyons

Hetton Lyons Colliery. In the nineteenth century there were three major tragedies following explosions at the pit. Twenty were killed in 1836, twenty-nine killed in 1845 and twenty-two in 1860. The colliery was closed in 1950 with the loss of 430 jobs.

The Hetton Lyons Lodge Banner outside the Half Moon Hotel at the Durham Miners' Gala in 1950. On the banner is a poster asking: 'The NCB has CLOSED our colliery Y?'

Sherburn

Loading wagons at Sherburn Hill Colliery around 1908. At this time the colliery was part of the Lambton Collieries group but was later sold to Dorman, Long & Co. In 1934 they employed 1,131 workers at the pit.

Inside the canteen at Sherburn Hill Colliery in 1949. The canteen was replaced soon after this photograph was taken.

In The Office
by Lena Cooper

I started working for the National Coal Board in 1955, in the Mechanisation Department situated at that time in Stockton Road, Sunderland. My immediate 'Boss' – the one I actually worked for – was George Renwick who was in charge of the mechanisation of the local mines. Machinery was taking over a lot of the hard back-breaking work of the miners. A mining revolution! He had a team of men to help organise and get this system working.

Then one morning the Senior Clerical Officer showed me an internal staff circular he had just received, asking for applications for a clerical vacancy in the Chairman's Office. Wow! The Chairman's Office at that time was in the National Coal Board Offices in Milburn House, Newcastle. He suggested that I should apply for the vacancy (in his view this position was 'top of the tree'). After a lot of persuasion and careful thought, I finally applied for the vacancy. It was one of the best decisions I ever made. I was granted an interview and, when that special day arrived, I was almost a nervous wreck. But I got the job.

In those days I found it easier to park my car in Gateshead on open spare ground, then get a bus across the Tyne Bridge. It took only about five minutes to walk down from the bus stop to Milburn House near the Quayside.

The job itself was a very confidential one – I was privy to the sight of meeting papers which, at that time, contained some very secret information. I had to attach any relevant papers and minutes thereon to the new Board Papers, in order that the Chairman could quickly check any previous information on the particular subjects.

While still at Milburn House, and a short time after I started in the Chairman's office, the new Chairman, Dr William Reid took over. When we moved to Team Valley Trading Estate offices there were three of us who were Chairman's staff, his secretary, a typist and myself.

When any Board meetings or special meetings were held in the Boardroom we were designated to serve coffee to all members in the meeting. Three of the many VIPs who visited Dr Reid were: Lord Robens – Chairman of the National Coal Board from 1961 to 1971, a strong character at the time. Dr Bronowski – the intellectual thinker, a quiet-voiced man, gentle mannered. Sam Watson – of the National Union of Mineworkers, Durham Area, a pleasant 'man of the people'.

We all loved Dr Reid. If there is such a person – he was the perfect boss. He was a gentleman, kind understanding, helpful, appreciative, hard-working, a very clever man and greatly respected. When he received the honour of a CBE Award, we were all so proud of him. Some time later, when he received his knighthood, I was so full of pride knowing that for a number of years I had the privilege of working for Sir William Reid.

Lena Cooper (left) and Muriel Melville outside the Coal Board Offices at Team Valley Trading Estate in the 1960s.

Sir Wiliam Reid with, right to left, his secretary, Muriel Melville, confidential clerk, Lena Cooper, and typist, Lilian Richardson. Sir William was born in a mining community in Fife. It is said that when he was three years old he was smuggled into a pit by a deputy. After studying mining at Edinburgh University, he worked in the Scottish Coal Industry in the years before and after the Second World War. In 1957 he moved south of the border and became chairman of the NCB's Durham Division and then regional NCB boss. He retired from the NCB in 1969. He was known for his work in mine safety and introduced the first miners' safety helmet.

Sam Watson with members of the Silksworth Lodge in the mid 1960s. Sam, who started at Boldon Colliery when he was fourteen, was elected Agent for the Durham Miners' Association in 1936. He served for twenty-seven years until he retired in 1963.

The administrative staff of the Northumberland and Durham Division of the National Coal Board moved into their new offices at Team Valley Trading Estate, Gateshead, in the late 1950s. The number of staff at that time was 770 but by 1963 the number had reduced to 250.

In 1972 the offices had a new name – the North Eastern Regional Office of the National Coal Board. It was a decade of colliery closures in both Northumberland and Durham regions of the National Coal Board with consequent staff reductions.

By 1986/87 the offices were obsolete and in 1991 were finally closed. The buildings were later demolished. Some time after, the site was taken over and a large Safeway store built. This was opened in February 1995. The store is on what is known as Coal House Roundabout.

Cornsay

A postcard of Cornsay Colliery from 1912. It was sent from 29$^{1}/_{2}$ Commercial Street, Cornsay Colliery to Middlesex. The postcard was produced by Mr Coates of Willington, a well-known and much respected photographer in the region. The colliery was closed in 1953.

Sinkers at Cornsay. Note the typical sinkers' headgear and capes.

Waterhouses

Waterhouses Colliery – one of a number of pits in the Deerness Valley. It was a Pease Company Pit, who in the mid 1860s built a 'model colliery village' to house their workers. Each house in the village had its own pig stye. Many pitmen kept animals and grew vegetables to help feed their families. The colliery was closed in 1966.

A group of men at Waterhouses Colliery. Written above the man in the centre is: 'This man is 97 years old.'

Lambton, Hetton & Joicey

In the 1920s the Lambton, Hetton & Joicey Company gave this account of how important coal preparation needed to be in a competitive market:

'Present day conditions demand that coal should be marketed in the cleanest possible condition. With this end in view the Company has spared neither pains nor money in equipping the various collieries with modern screening plant and both wet and dry cleaners.

In order that the most complete data respecting quality may be available, a thoroughly up-to-date Chemical Laboratory is maintained at the collieries. This is in the charge of an analytical chemist helped by a competent staff. Frequent and careful analyses are made, which enables the management to keep in daily touch with the products of the various pits and seams.'

The Lambton Chemical Laboratory.

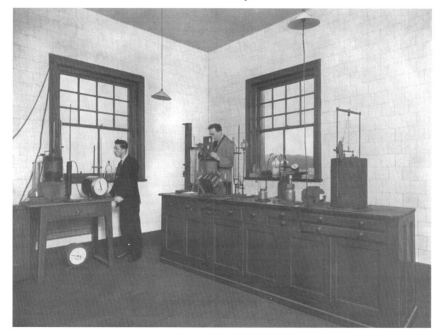

Coal washer, dry cleaner and washed coal storage bunker at Newbottle Colliery.

Cleaning belts and screens for large coal at Elemore Colliery.

Cleaning belts and screens for large and unscreened coal at Eppleton Colliery.

Sacriston

Sacriston Colliery. The Victory Pit at Sacriston was sunk in 1839 and mining continued in the village until 1985. When the colliery closed, the last ponies still working in the Durham Coalfield left the pit for the final time. There was also mining at nearby Charlaw and Witton.

A mobile conveyor loading trucks at Sacriston.

Shield Row Drift, Sacriston. Closed in the 1940s after operating for over 40 years.

Sacriston Colliery and Brick Works, around 1900.

Officials

Officials at Willie Pit, South Derwent Colliery, 20th September 1904. Colliery officials were overmen, deputies and chief clerks.

Hedley Pit Officials. The boilers behind them were made by Dunston Engine Works of Gateshead.

Officials at Hetton Lyons
Colliery. The man seated, second
right, is holding a shot firer's
lamp with a moveable guard.
The others are holding tin can
Davey Lamps.

Colliery official outside
Burnopfield Colliery Office,
around 1910. He is wearing the
traditional leather 'skull cap'
with the peak at the rear. Note
the boot scraper to the right.

Ryhope

An early view of Ryhope Colliery. After the colliery closed in 1966 the Department of Employment and Productivity compiled a study titled, *Ryhope: A Pit Closes*. In the publication, miners described how they felt about their employment at the pit coming to an end. Some of the men gave these comments:

'I cried when I got home.'

'I felt as if the bottom had been knocked out of my world; I have been at Ryhope for 44 years. I really didn't know what was going to happen.'

'I felt terrible: the thought of leaving the lads I knew and the place I was used to.'

'I didn't like the idea of having to move. Ryhope was a family pit.'

Ryhope Colliery fire brigade, around 1910.

Silksworth

New winding gear being installed at Silksworth Colliery in the 1950s. Less than twenty years later the colliery had closed.

The death pangs of Silksworth Colliery in the early 1970s – when it should have been celebrating just over a century of producing coal. Like many former colliery sites, the land where the pit once stood has been cleared and is used for leisure purposes.

Workers

Louisa Pit Mechanics, 1900.

Above: Three men carefully posed in the windinghouse at Elemore Colliery.

Right: In the boilerhouse at Handen Hold Colliery. On the right is Bob Lawson.

Winding engine men at Chilton Colliery in the 1920s.

George Short, shifter at Garesfield Colliery, Vesting Day 1947. George was born in 1872 and started work underground at Kimblesworth in 1884. When this photograph was taken he said: 'I am working regular for to help Shinwell. I have never worked out of Durham. I have worked 51 years at Garesfield Pit, High Spen, and still hope to help in production.' Behind him is a poster saying: 'Give him a hand to work safely. He's only a lad'. George died in 1960.

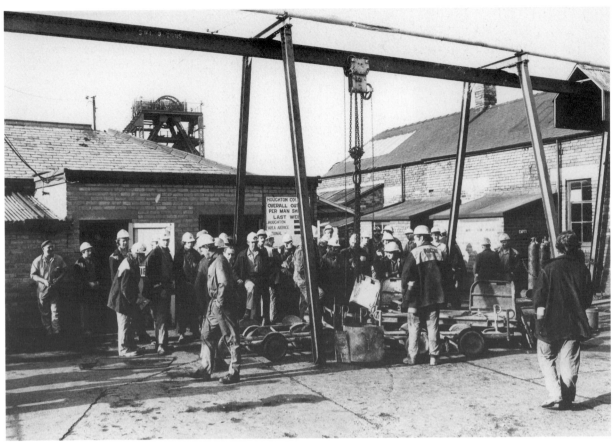

Outside the lamp cabin on the day of the last shift at Houghton Colliery, 24th April 1981.

Sinkers at Brusselton in 1906. Looks as if it's time to change the horses over.

A group of workers in the Pelton area, including electricians, fitters and mechanics. In the back row, second right, is Bob Magee a colliery electrician.

George Westgarth, former blacksmith at Eppleton Colliery. The photograph was taken at the Bowes Railway, Springwell in 2001 where George was exhibiting some of his sculptures inspired by his work in mining.

Chester Moor

A postcard of Chester Moor Colliery, from before 1910. The pit was located south of Chester-le-Street between the main Durham to Newcastle railway line and the old A1 (now A167). As you travelled these routes on a damp day you would inhale the sulphur smell of the burning pit heap. The colliery was closed in 1967.

Miners at Chester Moor around 1900. Note the man on the left has three picks on one shaft. One would be in use with the other two sharp to save coming up the shaft to get a pick sharpened. The official and the man sitting on the right are holding powder tins.

Stella and Dunston

This rare photograph was taken by postcard publisher R. Johnston of Gateshead in his 'Monarch Series', many of which are featured in this book. To the right of the head gear, across the River Tyne, can be seen the smoking chimneys of John Spencer & Sons' Newburn Steel Works.

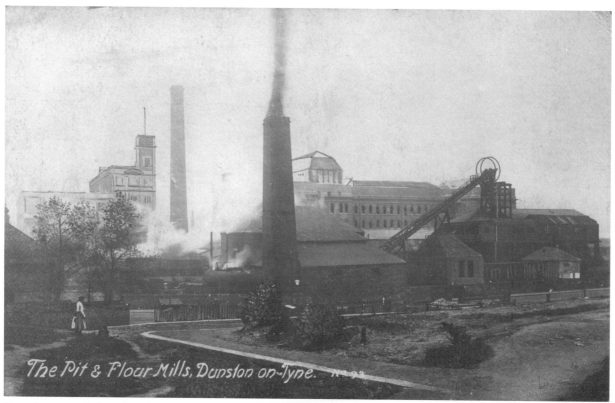

The Pit & Flour Mills, Dunston on-Tyne.

On the south bank of the River Tyne around 1908, Dunston Colliery and the nearby Co-operative Flour Mills.

Durham Miners' Hall

The Miners' Hall on North Road Durham. A postcard sent in July 1909. The hall had been opened in June 1876 with a council chamber holding over 250. Four statues – of Alexander MacDonald, William Crawford, William Patterson and John Foreman – were later erected on the windows of the hall. Alexander MacDonald was the President of the Miners' National Association while Crawford, Foreman and Patterson were early pioneers of the Durham Miners' Association. These men strived to change the working conditions of miners and fought for social injustice. This fight was carried on by many in later years. Today the NUM continues to campaign for the rights of miners – both past and present. The deep coal mines of Durham may be gone but there are still the after effects of the industry. In particular, there are many men who suffer the diseases and injuries caused by mining. Their suffering is a constant reminder of the price paid for coal.

The statue of William Crawford is unveiled in 1892. Thirteen years later the Durham Miners' Association moved its headquarters to Red Hills.

The Durham Miners' Hall and Agents Houses at Red Hills were opened 23rd October 1915. In the programme for the official opening of Red Hills there is a proud description of the hall:

'The building is in the Georgian style, and is line with the best tradition of English Classical Architecture. The facing is executed partly in ashlar stone and partly in pressed brick. The front facade is over 160 ft in length … In the centre of the roof is a large dome springing from an octagonal drum. The dome is finished with an octagonal turret and the whole is covered with copper … On opening the entrance doors we enter a Lobby and are faced with a fine executed oak screen with swing doors in same leading to the Entrance Hall. The Entrance Hall is paved with white, black and green marbles worked into panels, and the staircase is executed in white marble and finished with an artistically worked wrought-iron balustrade and oak handrail.

At the rear of the Entrance Hall, and entered by swing doors from Lobbies adjoining same, is the Council Hall, which is 61ft long, 49ft wide and 30ft high … The Council Hall is fitted with oak seats and desks providing accommodation (including Gallery) for nearly 400 delegates.'

A view of Red Hills showing one of the statues moved from the old hall on North Road.

Greenside

Greenside Colliery, Ryton. The colliery closed in 1966 after over a decade of decline. In 1957 there were 425 working underground with 100 above – less than half the figure from just after the war.

Greenside Colliery lamp cabin. They are Protector 'Type 6' lamps, still being made at Eccles near Manchester. When the pits were closed thousands of lamps were destroyed or simply thrown down the shafts. Now pit lamps are treasured collectors' items.

Wardley & Heworth

A group of men and boys in front of Follonsby Pit, Wardley. Gordon Stridiron, in his book *A History of Wardley, Its Colliery and People*, gives this early account of the pit:

'The sinking of Follonsby Colliery started on 30th September 1907 by Bowes and Partners and Follonsby Terrace was built and temporarily housed the sinkers. The East Boldon firm of sinkers, James Johnson and Sons Ltd, originally built 8 houses in the Terrace when they were awarded the contract on 7th November 1907. Bricklayers were paid at the hourly rate of 1s per hour and labourers 8d an hour. The houses were completed by August 1908 and cost £1,806 13s or approximately £225 per house. In later years, a larger, bay windowed house was built on both ends of the street, they housed the pit manager and the colliery engineer.'

Heworth Fanny Pit. One of three shafts at Heworth – the others being the John and Ada Shafts. The pit was closed in 1963.

Coke Works

Coke workers at Waldridge with their distinctive coke forks.

Whinfield Coke Works at Rowlands Gill around 1955. The coke ovens were filled with small coal from hand propelled trucks along the top of the ovens.

Two views of Whinfield Coke Works. Coke was removed from the oven and deposited on the flat bench by mean of a 'peel' hung from a pivoted crane.

Workers at Tanfield Coke Works with chaldrons above them for dropping coal into the ovens. Luke Harker told the story of when he lived at Oxhill and had to walk to Tanfield Coke Works, all the lads would meet up at Oxhill Arch and walk to work together. At night, tramps used to sleep around the coke ovens to keep warm and would set upon an individual to pinch his bait.

A new boiler is delivered to Browney Coke Works near Meadowfield. Today you would have few problems using hydraulic telescopic cranes with a large outreach to place the boiler on its plinth. But as you can see it was a case of 'jack and pack' on timber builds and the only assistance would be from hand operated winches.

Two more modern and larger Coke Works at Lambton (*above*) and Derwenthaugh (*right*).

In 1974 the Chairman of the National Coal Board, Derek J. Ezra, predicted a bright future for the Coke Works in the North East:

'Three of the North East's six NCB coking plants – Norwood, Derwenthaugh and Lambton – are pioneers of the technique developed locally by Board scientists in co-operation with our central research establishment, of blending coking coals of which Durham supplies a half of the national requirement. This ensures supplies of these coals, and of other coking reserves in the area, well into the next century, while also giving the market an eminently acceptable product.'

Horden, Blackhall & Shotton

The Colliery, Horden. 4228

Two views of Horden Colliery. A Horden Collieries Ltd promotion booklet of 1929 gave this description of Horden Colliery: 'This is the largest colliery in the group and the output has reached over 6,600 tons in one day, probably the largest quantity drawn at any colliery in the British Isles … Special facilities for riding the men to the Coal Face are provided in the Hutton Seam. These enable the men to start fresh and save travelling time.'

In 1929 Horden Collieries Ltd gave this account of their housing record in the area:

'When operations were commenced at Horden in the year 1900 there were neither railways, main roads nor houses; even water for steam-raising had to be carted. Today there is an up-to-date township of 14,000 inhabitants. Altogether the Company has built more than 3,000 houses and spent over £750,000 in this respect. In addition a considerable number have been built by the local Council and private builders.

Facilities have been provided by the Company to enable those men who wish to own their own houses to purchase them on easy terms by weekly payments. Streets, houses and business premises are all provided with electricity from the colliery mains. The domestic water supply for Horden and Blackhall is also provided by the Company from their own reservoirs.'

In the 1920s the company also had collieries at Blackhall, Shotton and Castle Eden. Here is Blackhall Colliery which first began to draw coals in 1914. The colliery closed in 1981.

Shotton was Horden Collieries' first pit. It was sunk in 1840 and was worked for 36 years before being abandoned. It was re-opened in 1900 and survived for a further 72 years.

Shotton Colliery in its final days. *Above*: The North Pit Engine House in 1971. *Below*:
Shotton Colliery from the south, around 1970.

Whitburn

Sinking started at Whitburn in July 1874 and the first coal was won in May 1897. The first death occurred at the pit when a sinker was killed in the shaft. In 1911 the Marsden Lodge of the Durham Miners' Association published a book of 'Prices and Conditions' at Whitburn Pit. The book also gave a 'list of fatal accidents, although incomplete, will give some idea of the human sacrifices made at Whitburn (Marsden) Colliery.'

Whitburn Pit in the early 1960s. In the foreground is the passenger platform used by the 'Marsden Rattler' until 1953.

Between 1890 and 1911 there were 68 deaths at the pit, including 15 boys. Just a brief snapshot in time in the history of the Durham Coalfield which shows the high price that was paid for coal. An agreement at the colliery in 1899 allowed widows to occupy their colliery houses for two months after the death of their husbands. If the family did not vacate the house after two months they were charged 5 shillings a week for rent and coals.

Whitburn Colliery in 1968 – the year the pit closed – with a NCB Hunslet diesel loco in the foreground.

A State Of The Art Pit

Over 1,000 years of coal production in County Durham came to an end when the last deep-coal mine, Wearmouth Colliery, closed in 1993. Through the many struggles and subsequent hardship of the miners, throughout the ages, the industry has slowly improved the working conditions. The hard daily toil was gradually reduced by the introduction of mechanisation and electrification into the mines. The industry has gone from 'coal at any price' to a business based on 'costs per Giga joule'. Global markets and the relative economics has been blamed for the shut down of our great industry. Because 'Durham was built on coal' the closure of the industry affected everyone in the county. The price of coal has been high in human terms, with many lives lost throughout the centuries, not to mention the many industrial diseases which last a lifetime. The efforts of the coal miners of Durham should never be forgotten. The heritage of a 'job for life' has gone forever, but we pay a tribute to all miners, with a selection of photographs of mineworkers in the last deep-coal mine in the county.

The pictures show how far the industry had modernised and improved, culminating in a state of the art pit with the use of the latest technology and a competent workforce, but unfortunately closed down as uneconomic.

Control Room Desk at Wearmouth.

The control room played an important role in the management of a modern coal mine, it was the hub of all pit activities, and was manned continuously 24 hours per day, seven days a week.

A vast array of monitoring equipment terminated at the control room desk, these were usually graphic displays, based on real time, and incorporated associated alarm systems. The equipment being monitored would include: the coal clearance system which included conveyors, bunkerage and coal drawing, the Mine Ventilation and methane drainage systems, minewater pumping systems were also monitored.

All communications throughout the mine were linked into the control room, giving direct access to coal faces and development drivages.

The controllers were usually astute pitmen with a good working knowledge and practical experience in methods of underground operations. A record was kept in the control room of all activities associated with production and safety at the mine.

The photographs show a typical underground, archgirded roadway with lagging of wood, with mesh panels. These roadways primarily accessed the thick coal seam and supplied the ventilation and could also include a belt conveyor to carry the coal.

The roadway would invariably incorporate a set of rail tracks to accommodate the transportation of materials by a transport system (rope haulage system shown). The white appearance of the roadway is due to the spread of stonedust. Other services running along the side of the roadway are: steel pipes for fresh water supply and minewater pumping, signal and power supply cables.

It can also be noted that conveyor belt manriding was in use, with men riding inbye on the bottom strand and the top strand of the conveyor was available for men riding outbye. It can be seen that rail track was laid to an improved standard by utilising steel sleepers and spring clips, not the wooden sleeper and dog spikes which had been previously in use.

Underground arched roadway.

Underground roadway with manriding on the conveyor.

Large conveyor systems were installed to give increased coal-carrying capacity. These were high horsepower installations with intricate start-up procedures to give gradual loading, and the ability to handle belt stretch, since some of the conveyors were thousands of metres long. Methods of monitoring conveyor tracking and roller conditions were improved by the use of temperature guns. When directed at the rollers an increased temperature may indicate roller failure, but could also indicate increased loading which may subsequently require tracking adjustment of the conveyor. These conveyors were the arteries of the mine and, together with strategically positioned bunkers, gave large storage capacity underground.

Huwood conveyor drive and loop-take-up unit.

Monitoring conveyor rollers (this photograph was taken at Dawdon Colliery).

Underground Roadway Drivage (Development)

Overman showing height of the coal seam.

The drivage rates of underground roadways was improved by a change of design in roadway support. Initial investigations and load testing of strata conditions underground revealed a new method of roadway support using 'Australian Roofbolt technology' could be adopted.

Full approval for the use of this new system of support took several months to gain. It was obtained by staged approval, with roadway support going through a combination of support methods until the final stage of the whole roadway, roof and sides fully bolted using fibre glass bolts and thin steel straps.

One man drilling the roof with Wombat machine.

Two men drilling roof for roof straps.

Joy Continuous Miner at a junction underground. The development roadways were driven by continuous miners each initially backed up with a shuttle car system. The system was subsequently changed to eliminate the shuttle car, and the miners loaded out directly on a walking conveyor.

Bolted roadway with timber supports.

The development roadway shows an early stage of approval by using roofbolting techniques with timber supports. A water barrier can be seen up at roof level, this replaced the stone dust barrier system for preventing propagation of a coal dust explosion. Ventilation tubing can be clearly seen in the top corner of the roadway, this was required whilst the roadway was being driven.

Development team with undermanager and overman.

Left: Development team on drilling.

Below: Development drivage record breakers.

The efforts of the workmen was tremendous, despite the new machinery and methods of work being used, they learned quickly to overcome teething problems. This effort was acknowledged when development teams repeatedly set up new drivage records week after week.

Development team in roadway heading.

Coal Production

Driving roadways in thick-coal seams will produce a certain amount of coal, but the primary method of coal production was by long-wall production methods.

View along thin-seam coal face conveyor.

Thick-coal production by remotely operated shearer.

Prior to entry into the thick-coal seam, coal came from thin-seam longwall faces usually 250 yards long and between 3ft to 4ft thick. Coal was usually cut by ranging-arm shearers and loaded out on flexible face conveyors made of steel. The roof was supported by 180 tonne powered roof supports.

Undulating coal seams caused problems particularly in thin-seam working, these were greatly reduced when mining the thicker-seams. The workmen were forced to crawl about on hands and knees in the thin-seams all the shift, whilst the thick-seams allowed remote operation of the machine from an upright position. These improved conditions were reflected in the production from the face in the thick-coal, beating all previous production records for the whole of the pit.

Workman reaching for control handle on heavy duty powered support.

Thick-coal seams bring their own particular difficulties. Equipment was much larger and heavier, and indeed some of the control handles on the new generation of roof supports were just reachable. Equipment needed safe, careful handling and transportation, the use of locomotive haulage gave the greater flexibility when handling these loads.

A new generation of rubber-tyred battery locomotives gave greater adhesion to the track, and ability to negotiate steeper gradients.

Manriding to these undersea workings was provided by trains headed by diesel locomotives.

Underground rubber-tyred battery locomotive hauling a powered roof support.

Underground diesel locomotive and manriding car.

A view of Wearmouth Colliery from the River Wear.

With the production of coal, invariably came unwanted waste. The disposal of this waste was by the use of barges. The waste was loaded directly from the washery into the barges via the staithes on the River Wear. The barges used were called *Bumble Bee 1* and *Bumble Bee 2* and carried the waste down river and out into the North Sea, beyond the three mile limit.

Wearmouth Colliery was a long established deep-coal mine off the coast at Sunderland. Near to the end of its working life it still held treasures from long ago. This picture shows an old boiler discovered near the bottom of one of the shafts by two shaftsmen. At first glance it looks like a submarine has just pushed through the ice under the polar ice cap.

Final Days

The demolition of Wearmouth Colliery in the 1990s.

Seaham Colliery in the early 1990s. Seaham was merged with Vane Tempest in the 1980s and was gradually run down until the site was cleared shortly after this photograph was taken.

Vane Tempest, June 1993, just after closure. The pit was demolished a year later.

Kevin Mould in front of the 'Miners' Lamp' outside the Stadium of Light – once the site of Wearmouth Pit.

RAILWAYS

A coal train approaches Durham from the Bishop Auckland area in the early 1960s. The engine is a Q6 0-8-0, one of the workhorses of the North East coalfield.

A 4ft 2in gauge wagonway made of wood which was discovered buried beneath coal dust and slurry on the site of the former Lambton Coke Works. The wagonway is believed to date from the late 1700s and was photographed in March 1996. Frank Atkinson, in his book *The Great Northern Coalfield*, gives this account of the early wagonways: 'In the mid 17th century, wooden wagonways were laid over which wheeled vehicles could more easily be drawn. This

was a great improvement on the muddy, often almost impassable cart ways, and a horse could pull a large four-wheeled wagon, usually holding about 2 tons. Two sets of wooden rails were laid, and in descending one track the driver hitched his horse to the rear of the wagon, unless the descent was too gradual for the wagon to travel by its own weight: in ascending the other track the animal pulled back the empty vehicle … By 1700 coal was frequently carried 8 or 10 miles to the Tyne from collieries at Tanfield, Pontop and South Moor and it was not until the 19th century when the steam railway again reduced the costs of carriage that collieries were sunk much further inland.'

An engine at Lambton Coke Works filling with water. The water was softened to take out any lime. Engine No 45, 0-6-0 saddle tank, was built by Hawthorn Leslies in 1912 and was in service for over 50 years before being scrapped in 1970.

An electric engine at Westoe. These electric engines were very effecient, requiring a lot less maintenance than their coal-powered counterparts.

The NCB Harton System. Electric locomotive 13 at Harton Low Staithes with shale from Westoe Colliery in April 1988. Westoe ceased production in May 1993.

Lambton Engine Works

Engine and wagons outside the loco sheds at Lambton Engine Works at Philadelphia. The Philadelphia works was the biggest of its kind in Durham and in its heyday had two to three thousand workers employed in wagon shops, a foundry, boiler shop, plate shop, saw mill, paint shop and fitting shop.

Taking a break with an engine from Philadelphia: B. Adamson, D. Baggott, M. Pitt, H. Bowden, J. Avery, J. Morrell, J. Evans and J. Byron. Engines such as this would often have a lovely clean shovel which was used as a frying pan.

T. Speed, N. Robson, M. Pitt and A. Campbell outside the railway office at Lambton Engine Works in 1985.

Two engines in the sheds at Philadelphia in August 1966.

The last brass cast at Lambton Engine Works in October 1985.

The last cast iron casting at Lambton Engine Works in October 1985.

An engine pulling a train of coal wagons at Penshaw in the 1960s. Tom Hardy, who worked on the railways for many years, explains how an order would be placed for coal and how the railway system would implement this:

'Imagine a boat is waiting at Sunderland Drops for an order of 50,000 tons of washed doubles. Engines would be sent to the local colliery – such as Houghton or the Dolly Pit at Philadelphia – to pick up the washed doubles they had which would be then transported to the Penshaw sides. This was repeated at other neighbouring collieries until there was enough to make up a train which would then run to Sunderland. It was important to get this order down to Sunderland before the tide changed.'

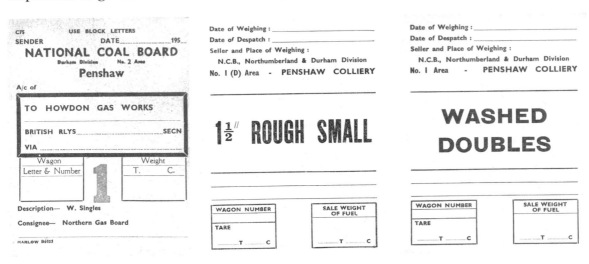

Wagon labels which were put on railway trucks to indicate the weight, type of coal and destination. Washed doubles was the best coal and used overseas or shipped to London. Rough small was used in power stations.

Tom Hardy (manager) presents Jack Hood with his retirement present at Seaham Wagon Works. Jack was a wagon examiner at Dawdon Colliery.

Tom Hardy's retirement presentation at Seaham Wagon Works in 1983. At the time of his retirement, Tom was Area Railway Workshop Manager. He had started in the industry in 1938 as an apprentice wagonwright at Philadelphia. He worked his way up to become chargehand and then in charge of Hetton Wagonshops in 1952. He moved on to Seaham and was made foreman in 1963 and then manager in 1973. In this photograph are, left to right: Dave Valks, Morris Doughty, Harry Chapman, Bob Wood, Bob Copeland, Tom Hardy, unknown, Mary Hardy, Jim Steele, Maureen Elliott, Fred Weakly and unknown. They all worked at Seaham Wagonworks.

Lambton Drops

Lambton Drops, Sunderland.

The book *Sketches Of The Coal Mines In Northumberland And Durham* gives this early account of the drops at Sunderland:

'The first staithes for the *shipment* of coals on the Wear were erected on the site displayed in 1812, when three sprouts were opened. The railways were brought to the western rink of a deep ravine, called 'Galley's Gill', where an extensive depot was erected; and a strong bridge of timber, at a considerable inclination, was laid across the Gill, forming an inclined plane, down which the wagonway was passed, and through a tunnel in a projecting rock to the sprouts. The erection of these works caused a considerable sensation amongst the keelmen and casters of the Wear, then, for the first time, forced into competition with shipping staithes; and, several similar establishments having been talked about, on the afternoon of March 20, 1815, a great number of persons, chiefly belonging to the above professions, assembled in a riotous manner, and preceded to pull down the wooden bridge, which they effected by means of ropes. They also set fire to the depot and machinery for lowering the waggons down the inclined plane; and one house in the neighbourhood was pulled down, and several others unroofed. Many persons were injured by the falling timbers, and one man was killed. At a late hour in the night, a party of dragoons arrived from Newcastle, and dispersed the mob. The injury was estimated at £6,000.'

Engine NCB 0-6-2T 30 and brakevan passes Pallion Station on its way from Lambton Staithes to Penshaw Yard, 22nd April 1963. The engine was built by Kitson's of Leeds in 1907 and was scapped in 1969.

At Lambton Staithes, Sunderland, an engine takes water outside the shed while another shunts wagons in August 1964.

NCB 0-6-2T 42 at Penshaw North with coal empties for Harraton Colliery in August 1964.

A coal train leaves South Pelaw and heads towards Consett, 24th August 1966.

A Rumanian-built engine smothers the area with exhaust fumes as it leaves Wearmouth Colliery with a south-bound merry-go-round coal train in April 1985.

A snowplough-fitted engine passes Monkwearmouth Railway Museum with empty wagons for Wearmouth Colliery, April 1985.

A Barclay diesel 623 leaves Hilda Sidings with empty wagons for Westoe Colliery, April 1988. Electric loco 12 is in the background.

Wardley Coal Disposal Point in May 1989.

Returning from Pesspool to Murton with empty wagons, Barclay 0-6-0 DH crosses the bridge over the A182 road at South Hetton, July 1989.

A Wagon tippler at Pesspool, near South Hetton, July 1989. Here colliery waste from the Murton area was transferred to road vehicles for dumping in Tuthill Quarry.

A Life On The Railways

M. Pitt, T. Hayes and J. Robson in 1953. Morris Pit started in the running sheds where he would clean tubes and fire boxes, before moving on to be a guard, then a fireman and later a driver.

Morris Pitt driving an engine at the North Yorkshire Railway at Pickering in 1999.

Morris Pitt (shunter) with, on the right with his back turned, Norman Lee (fireman) and, on the left, Jack Swainston (driver) at Houghton in 1967.

A group of enthusiastic volunteers in front of the Lambton Worm (No 29) at North Yorkshire Railway in 1999. This was a mainline engine which worked the line from Penshaw to Sunderland. It was based at the Lambton Engine Works and would draw coals at Penshaw and take them to the drops at Sunderland. Some of the volunteers pictured here worked at Philadelphia and standing on the platform is Andrew Robinson who used to drive the engine when it was working in Durham.

WARTIME

Members of the Bevin Boys' Association march down the Mall during the VJ Day Parade in 1995.

The Forgotten Conscripts of The Second World War
by Warwick Taylor

These men could well be described as having served in a secret underground movement, but not in the sense that most of us imagine, for the majority of people today have never heard of the term Bevin Boy.

From December 1943 until the end of the war, 47,859 Bevin Boys, so named after Ernest Bevin, the wartime Minister of Labour and National Service, were directed to work underground in the coal mines. The unpopular decision became necessary in order to meet production demands vital to the war effort and, in order to do this, an additional 50,000 men would have to be conscripted over a period of eighteen months.

The system employed by the Minister was that of a ballot scheme whereby young men of call-up age, upon registering would be selected according to the last digit of his registration number. Draws were made at fortnightly intervals by the Minister's Secretary. The fact of having completed pre-service training in a Cadet Force would not be considered grounds for exemption. Not all Bevin Boys were ballotees, as the unballoted were given the opportunity in lieu of service in the Armed Forces and were classified as Optants or Volunteers. They were not Conscientious Objectors.

After medical examinations, travel warrants and instructions would follow to report to one of the thirteen Government Training Centre Collieries in the United Kingdom. Upon arrival at the assigned destination, a Ministry of Labour Official would be waiting to allocate accommodation in either a Miners' Hostel similar to an army camp or in private billets the cost of which was 25 shillings per week which was deducted from an average wage of three pounds ten shillings.

Training would last for a duration of four weeks involving physical training, with classroom, surface and underground work. Bevin Boys were supplied with a safety helmet, a pair of overalls and steel capped boots and, like other miners, carried a safety lamp, a snap tin containing sandwiches and a water bottle. After the initial training period, allocation would be made to work at a colliery usually within the same area

Bevin Boys training at Cramlington Lamb Colliery in Northumberland.

where the training took place and again accommodation would be either in a hostel or private billets.

All Bevin Boys worked underground and were usually employed on conveyor belts or the loading and haulage of tubs using machinery or pit ponies. The work was hard, often in appalling conditions, working in cramped spaces and having to walk considerable distances from the pit bottom over uneven terrain in areas that were either hot, cold, wet, draughty, dirty, dusty and smelly. The constant noise of machinery was also deafening, coupled with the daily hazards of enduring cuts and bruises and the ever present risk of explosion and fire caused by firedamp or methane gas or rock falls. There were no toilet facilities. Some of the larger collieries were lucky enough to have pithead baths in order to shower and change into clean clothes, but where these were not provided it would mean going back to the hostel or billets.

But how did the Bevin Boy rate with his fellow miners who were suddenly faced with an invasion of young inexperienced men with little knowledge of the industry? It was understandable that a certain amount of suspicion fell upon these newcomers who had come from all walks of life, many of whom had never got their hands dirty in their lives. Regular miners, many of whom were born and bred in a mining community, relied on bonuses earned by hard work, would not relish the idea of working alongside a Bevin Boy who showed a complete lack of interest and did not pull his weight. Fortunately, these fears and suspicions were soon dispelled, proving their capability.

The Bevin Boy did not have a uniform and therefore, only wore civilian clothes when off duty. Small wonder that this attire attracted public attention prompting adverse remarks as to why they were not in uniform of the Forces. Being of military age, invited frequent challenging by local police on suspicion of being a draft dodger, deserter or even a possible enemy agent.

With the ending of the war in Europe, eventually a release scheme was introduced similar to that of the Forces, but Bevin Boys received no other form of recognition or reward for their services to the war effort in which they played a very vital part. I served as a Bevin Boy in South Wales and have never lost respect for the miner, but I am determined that the role of the Bevin Boy will not be excluded from the history of the Nation. In recent years, a National Bevin Boys Association has been formed with a current membership of over 1,500 and we always welcome new members.

Members of the Bevin Boys' Association at the Bescot Stadium, Walsall, in 1998. Warwick Taylor is in the front row to the left of the banner.

A group of Bevin Boys at Morrison Busty in October 1944. Fourth from the left is Gerry Moore who was killed in the Louisa Morrison Colliery disaster on 23rd August 1947.

The Memorial Stone at Annfield Plain for the Louisa Morrison Disaster. Gerry Moore and F.E. Martin were both Bevin Boys.

Wearmouth At War
by Peter Gibson

Miners at Wearmouth caused uproar in 1941 when they refused to work during air raids. Peter Gibson looks at the background to the dispute.

Wearmouth Coal Company had an arrangement with the Royal Observer Corps that when enemy aircraft were within a certain radius a bell rang and red lights flashed at various parts of the colliery and miners went to the shelters. But on 24th December 1940, the Durham Miners' Association and the Northumberland and Durham Coal Owners' Association entered into an agreement that miners would work during air raid alerts so coal production would not be impeded.

However, on 21st July 1941, 1,250 Wearmouth miners unanimously decided to stop work at the pit during air raid alerts.

Although the site of the pit on the river and in close proximity to the shipyards made them a key industrial target in the front line for attack, their decision not to conform with other collieries in Durham and indeed with other coalfields in Britain where miners were working in alerts brought much criticism.

Their own leader, the President of the National Mineworkers' Federation, Will Lawther, denounced the Wearmouth miners' decision as 'an act of treason and cowardice'. And despite the miners' county leaders and their own lodge officials urging them to fall in line with the rest of the Durham Coalfield, Wearmouth miners remained adamant.

On 24th July, Wearmouth Miners' Lodge passed a resolution protesting against Mr Lawther's attack upon them, and a lodge spokesman, who wished to remain anonymous, put forward the miners' case.

He said: 'The argument for miners to work in air raid alerts should not have been entered into. The majority of lodges who carried the agreement are in comparatively safe areas in the county. To be blunt, they scarcely know what an air raid is. Any agreement that was made should have contained a promise that it should apply with modifications for collieries such as Wearmouth situated in vulnerable areas.

'We contend that the shaft and the winding arrangement are inadequate. Each of the two cages consists of two decks. One deck has to remain stationary with men crammed

Wearmouth Colliery.

into it, while the other is being loaded. It takes three or four minutes to come to bank.

'In each cage there are 24 men.

'In a shipyard or a factory, men get warned that a bomb is coming down and are able to dive for shelter We can do nothing but stand where we are, jammed in the cage unable to move a foot or an arm. We are determined that we won't work during alerts.'

A *Sunderland Echo* reporter asked the spokesman why their local and national leaders hadn't accepted Wearmouth miners' objections as genuine, and he replied: 'They are suffering from an excess of patriotic zeal. They made an agreement without bearing in mind the peculiar situation of a colliery such as Wearmouth, and now they have got to save their faces.'

Wearmouth miners' main concern was a direct hit on a shaft, or such bomb damage being done at the pithead that the engineman in control of the cage was put out of action, thereby putting miners' lives in jeopardy.

Pressure was put on the miners from all sides to work normally during air raids for the war effort. The *Echo* described the dispute as a mutiny and urged men to apply reason and common sense.

Wearmouth miners held several lodge meetings to discuss the matter, and they finally agreed to a ballot which took place on 26th August 1941, when two thirds of Wearmouth miners lodge members cast their votes.

The result was a majority of members in favour of working during air raid alerts. The figures were FOR 527, AGAINST 432.

Consequently, Wearmouth miners began working during alerts, but with the provision of two 'spotters' at the pithead.

The spotters were appointed, one by the miners and one by management, and it was their job to give warning of the approach of enemy aircraft.

Only then, and under the industrial warning system, could miners stop work and go to the shelters.

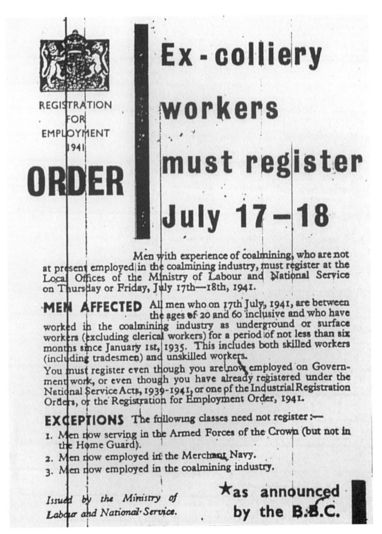

An advertisement from the *Sunderland Echo*, 16th July 1941, calling for ex-miners to register for work. No more miners were called up to the Armed Forces from 24th June 1941 because of the need for coal to help the war effort.

THE PRICE OF COAL

A Memorial postcard for the Glebe Colliery Explosion at Washington in 1908. Fourteen men were killed in the explosion and fire which followed. Thousands attended the funerals of the men killed in the disaster. For the funeral of three of the dead men – Messrs Wake, Cowan and Madden – 22,000 people formed a mile long cortege. The mourners had come from throughout Durham and Northumberland. Many were miners themselves and had come to pay their respects to their fellow pitmen.

Brancepeth 'A' Pit Disaster
by Olive Linge

Monday, 13th April 1896 was a normal working day at the 'A' Pit at Brancepeth Colliery. It was a pit employing over 300 men and boys and not as one would expect at Brancepeth but in Willington, a village just to the south west. The foreshift had completed their shift with the back shift following on and finishing at 4 pm.

It was then the turn of the stonemen and shifters, together with whatever officials were needed to repair and prepare the workings ready for the next day.

Around 10 pm (times vary according to whose account is told) Mr Mould, working in the engine house on bank, told of how he was sitting quite quietly when he heard a low peculiar noise. When interviewed he is reported as saying: 'I'll tell you what the noise was like. You have been sitting in your house at night when all is tranquil when suddenly you hear a gust of wind blowing against the door and making the trees moan in the distance, then in a moment all is still. That's what the noise was like.'

Determined to find out the cause, he went to inspect the boiler house but everything in there was normal. He then made his way towards the shaft to find that he was walking through a layer of dust 2-3 inches deep. Rising out of the shaft was more dust. Realising that something was dreadfully wrong he summoned the boiler man, and together they looked down the mouth of the shaft, where under normal circumstances lights could be seen, but to their dismay nothing was visible.

The alarm was raised and within a short space of time the Colliery Agent, Mr Weeks, and the Manager, Mr Grieves, were on the scene. Rescue parties were organised, with men from other collieries joining the local men later in the night. They were able to enter the pit by the shaft which was still intact.

On arriving at the shaft bottom it became clear to them that a major disaster had occurred. The explosion had originated far into the workings and the tubs which were waiting to take the foreshift to the coal faces had been blown to smithereens. Miraculously, two youths, Cunningham and Mullen, together with Mr Wilson, the lampman, who had been working at the shaft bottom, were relatively unscathed.

As the rescuers penetrated further, having gone about 300 yards, they came upon the first mangled body. Beyond this point, shouting could be heard and two youths, Bird and Blackett, who had been engaged in pumping operations just off the main workings, were found unhurt.

The force of the explosion having swept past them like a rush of wind, extinguishing their lights leaving them in total darkness. They had managed to find their way over a slight fall when they heard the voices of the rescue team. A happy end for another two.

The teams were soon stopped in their tracks by huge piles of debris and they had to painstakingly make their way moving rubble as they progressed. From time to time more bodies were discovered but several men still remained unaccounted for – and so they continued their thankless journey moving still further into the bowels of the earth.

During the rescue operations one overman, Mr Gilchrist, had a narrow escape when at the head of his team, he climbed over a fall and in so doing he toppled into one of the workings where there was a large accumulation of firedamp. His

Brancepeth 'A' Pit, Willington.

colleagues, by forming a human chain, managed to drag his unconscious body out. He was eventually taken to bank where he was attended by Dr Brown, a local GP, and eventually made a full recovery.

The scene at the pithead during the rescue operations. The picture was taken by a local photographer, Mr A. Alder.

In general the people of Willington were not immediately aware of the horror which dawn would bring. But as is usual with a disaster of this magnitude, when news did eventually circulate, a large crowd gathered at the pithead. They waited anxiously in dull rainy weather much in keeping with the sombre mood of relatives hoping for news of their loved ones.

The arduous task continued throughout the day but it was to be 7 pm before the first few bodies were brought to the surface encased in hastily prepared coffins which the colliery joiners had been working on all day.

By midnight another five bodies had been recovered. Two miles into the workings, extremely high levels of firedamp had accumulated, causing the rescuers to abandon their search whilst consultations took place on the most efficient way of directing fresh air into the area.

It was to be six days before the last body was recovered bringing the fatality total to seventeen men and three boys. Of these twenty persons only one had been killed outright by the explosion, the rest having died of carbon monoxide poisoning.

During these horrific days, tales of heroism emerged but every man who took part in the rescue mission was deemed a hero. Two of the rescued men, Cook and Harrison, had insisted on going back into the pit to help.

The women of the village also played their part, supplying huge amounts of refreshments daily. Their names: Mesdames, Hall, Hott, Pigdon, Gatiss, Marshall, Jackson and Kilburn. Misses Hall, Glenton, Hewitson, Robinson and Bradley.

In the aftermath of this disaster the people of Willington, a typical close knit community, gave their whole hearted support to the bereaved families providing whatever help was necessary to relieve their burden.

These men who gave their lives in the name of coal have not been forgotten and on the 100th anniversary of this tragedy a memorial service was held in the Wesleyan Chapel in Willington, attended by young and old alike.

When the Miners' Welfare Hall was built in Willington in 1926 a marble plaque was put in place as a lasting reminder of these brave men and boys.

The future location of this memorial is in some doubt but the people of Willington will make a united effort to ensure that it is erected in a place befitting its importance as part of its heritage.

The plaque on show in the entrance of the Miners' Welfare Hall.

Wingate Grange Colliery Disaster

On the 14th October 1906 an explosion ripped through Wingate Grange Colliery. A *Sunderland Echo* reporter was soon on the scene and gave this account of the disaster:

'What is considered as one of the most appalling disasters that has taken place in the colliery fields of Durham for many years occurred last night at about 20 minutes to twelve at Wingate. It has thrown the whole of the countryside and the populous colliery district of Wingate into a state of consternation. The explosion was felt with terrific force and it is stated that a number of buildings in the vicinity felt the force of the concussion so greatly as to receive damage. The shock was felt as far as the railway station, which is some distance from the pit.

The noise was deafening, and aroused the whole of the residents, the majority of whom were in bed. Thousands of persons, many of them half dressed, and all panic stricken rushed to the pithead, where there were scenes of great excitement, and the families of men who were known to be in the pit ran about making anxious enquiries. Rescue parties were soon formed and began their hazardous work.

This morning the whole of the district presented a sorrowful spectacle. Most of the shops were closed in consequence of the feeling that when the death toll was completed it would be a large one.

A touching incident is that connected with the man Harry Pace, who met his death in the five-quarter seam. He went back to assist a fellow worker but was overcome and collapsed. When reached by the exploring party he was able to speak to them, but he died before he was brought out.'

A later report stated: 'Harry Pace lost his life in an heroic attempt to rescue Broomfield. He had apparently been trying to drag Broomfield along when he was overcome by afterdamp. Another 20 yards and he would have been in fresh air.'

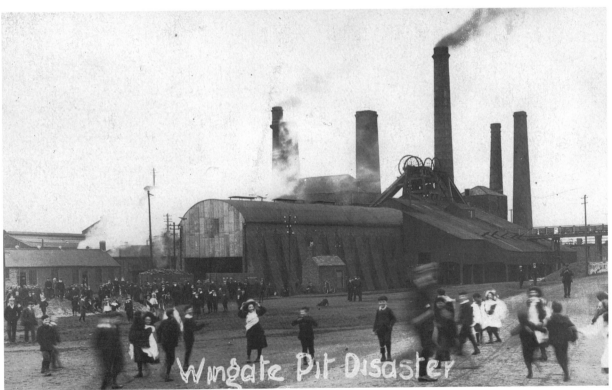

People rush to Wingate Colliery on the day of the disaster in 1906, when twenty-four were killed.

Rescue workers at Wingate.

The banner leads the funeral procession at Wingate a few days after the tragedy.

The *Sunderland Echo* reported the funerals in 'a village in deepest sorrow':

'The last act in Wingate's terrible tragedy was performed today when the victims of the disaster were taken to their final resting place. For days the place had something of the aspect of a village of the dead – so many of the houses were steeped in mourning. Each of the stricken homes had yesterday received its coffined dead, whose presence in the place had given deeper poignancy to the grief. Nature itself seemed to feel the gloom of the occasion and was, as it were, weeping in sympathy with the distress of her children.'

After the final burial: 'Slowly as the earth closed over the dead the crowd began to depart, grave and silent, their spirits saddened and chastened by the solemnity of the scene they had witnessed. The hush of death still hangs over the village.'

The Burns Pit Disaster

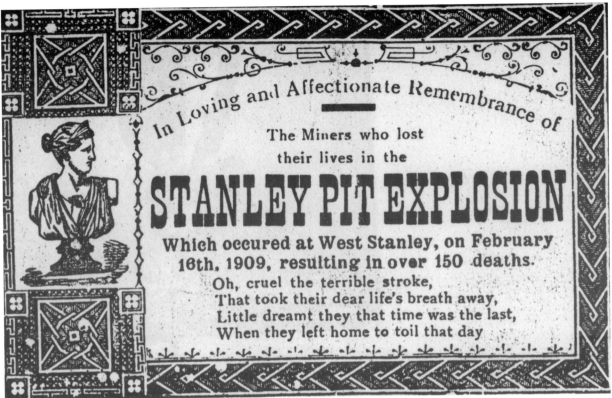

A memorial card for the West Stanley (Burns Pit) disaster of 1909. On Tuesday, 16th February 1909 two explosions sent flames shooting from the pit. A tragedy was beginning to unfold.

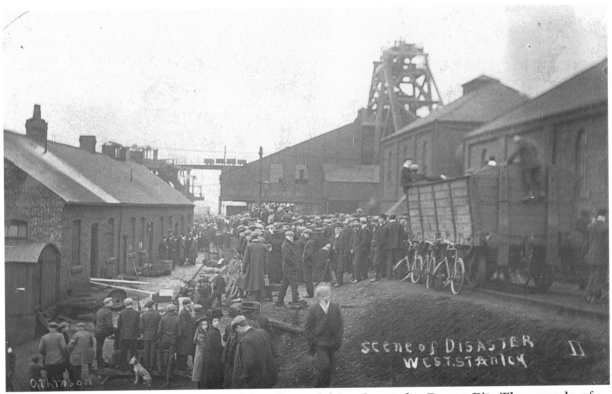

Crowds gather, waiting for news of family and friends, at the Burns Pit. Thousands of people made for the pit soon after the explosion to wait for news of loved ones. The disaster claimed the lives of 168 men and boys.

The burial of some of the victims of the disaster. It was estimated that 200,000 people came to the town of Stanley on the first day of the funerals. At one point the crowds were so great the funeral procession was unable to move for a time. Many of the victims were buried in mass graves at St Andrew's Church.

A postcard showing the 168 men and boys who lost their lives at West Stanley Colliery. Thirty survivors were led to safety from the pit. As well as postcard and memorial cards, there were also commemorative pit lamps sold after the disaster. They were made in Birmingham and sold to raise funds for bereaved families. There is some opinion that the lamps were made as prototypes for larger lamps and as they were surplus to requirements it was decided to sell them off.

William Gardner, one of the thirty survivors, rescued from the West Stanley disaster.

The Gospel Mission Hall at Witton Gilbert. Built by Langley Park miner, Jack Allen, in memory of the 168 miners who lost their lives at Stanley on 16th February 1909.

Easington Colliery Disaster
by Frank Ramsay

Frank Ramsay was a member of the Ashington Mines' Rescue Brigade from 1939 to 1953 and attended the Easington Colliery Disaster in 1951 when 81 miners and two rescue workers were killed. Here is his account of the tragedy.

Easington Colliery was a coastal pit with huge reserves of high quality coal that stretched way out under the North Sea. It is what was called a 'modern pit' with up-to-date coal cutting and coal loading machinery installed underground. The labour force totalled just over 2,700 men and boys.

The disaster occurred on 29th May 1951, when there were two shifts of men in the Duckbill district of the colliery – 43 men on the stone shift, who were due to finish work at 5.00 hours, and 38 men on the back shift, who had begun work at 3.30 hours.

Shaft rolley-way man Frank Leadbitter noticed thick dust and smoke, and promptly phoned the under manager, Mr Emery, at his home. He tried to make contact with the Duckbill district, but not being able to reach anyone, he walked inbye and met the fore-shift overman William Cook. They both went inbye and later thought that they heard a second explosion, probably one of the large falls of roof and sides. As the air was foul, they returned and phoned Mr Hopkins, the manager, who sent for the Mines' Rescue Brigade who arrived at 5.30 hours.

Houghton-le-Spring Mines' Rescue Station received a 'flash call' to say 'explosion at the Easington Colliery Duckbill district – 25 men affected'. As per brigade order, the three nearest rescue stations responded to the call – Houghton, Crook and Elswick – each station turning out their No 1 rescue tender, the superintendent, station officer and nine men. When they arrived at the pit, they were informed that the casualty figure could be as high as 50 men.

Meanwhile, Mr Frye, who was the area general manager, Mr Hopkins, Mr Emery and the fore-overman had proceeded inbye to a fall of roof and sides near the west main coal return airway, but were unable to go further because of gas. However, when the

Easington Colliery. A postcard posted 15th April 1914. The message reads: 'This is Easington Pit, showing the last big accident to the roof of the engine house, when the end of the winding rope lashed it off.' Easington was closed in 1993.

rescue teams descended the pit, it was obvious that they had a major disaster on their hands. So the emergency operation procedure was put into operation:

Flash calls to all collieries to mobilise their part-time rescue teamsmen.
Hospitals alerted, ambulance service, hospital and local doctors on call out register, police, mobile laboratory, unions notified.
Her Majesty's Inspector of Mines notified.
All leave cancelled.
The liquid oxygen plant started up, and all appliances to be loaded up.

Ashington Mines' Rescue Station was called out at 6.30 hours and arrived at the pit, 40 miles away, at 7.40 hours, with the superintendent, station officer and nine men in the No 1 rescue tender. We descended the pit with breathing apparatus at 8.15 am. Our air samples indicated a carbon monoxide content of 7.5 to 8%, so we assumed that the possibility of anyone being alive in such an atmosphere was nil. Because of this, most of the teams were assigned to restoring the ventilation, and clearing the falls of the roof and sides. We had to manhandle pit props, brattice cloth, and planks over falls and scattered machinery. The whole area was devastated, as though a bomb had exploded. Until the ventilation was restored, all of our air samples were lethal.

As all full-time rescue brigadesmen were put onto a 12 hour work shift system, I drew the short straw and was assigned the 12 midnight to 12 noon, plus travelling time each way, each day. Usually teams were made up as follows: team leader (myself), six part-time rescue teamsmen, plus one full-time rescue brigadesman who brought up the rear as vice-captain.

Bodies were strewn everywhere in ragged, burnt clothing. Machinery was scattered, some being lifted off course, loading points were up-ended, and machinery cases smashed open, with oil, grease and coal dust mixed up and splashed everywhere. The nearer we came to the Duckbill district, the worse it became. Many of the teamsmen were showing signs that they had had enough of the gory sights.

After days of work the National Coal Board became greatly concerned at the number of part-time rescue teamsmen who were showing signs of distress. Because of this, an order went out that all personnel engaged in rescue operations were to have a medical examination before proceeding underground. Many failed the test, with a result that rescue teams were depleted, and quite often, it became half regulars and half part-timers. Even then, many part-timers failed to turn up, until eventually the powers-that-

Fire and Rescue Station at Houghton-le-Spring.

be decided that in view of the distress of some, to call a halt to all rescue operations for 48 hours.

However, while this '48 hour cease-fire' was in operation, there was no let-up for the brigade. We had our station routine to carry out, the usual chores, call-outs to three surface fires, wash, hose and so on, running the liquid air plant, watch room duties etc. Those turning out to the pit were on such duties as air sampling or were engaged in repairing apparatus harness, soldering purifier cases, refilling ambulance boxes, even to replacing buckles on three stretchers. So it wasn't a 48 hour stand-down for the brigadesmen.

Even afterwards, we found many part-timers failing to turn up. For some it was their first and last sortie at an explosion of the magnitude of Easington Colliery. However, some grimly carried on. Being team leader, I had many teams under my direction, exploring, repairing roadway, clearing fall, gas and dust sampling, and the gruesome task of recovering the victims, often the bare remains of what was once a human being. I had some fine stout-hearted part-timers in my teams. They did a good job, and many thanks to them.

After seventeen days, all rescue operations ceased. We were glad to see the back of Easington Colliery.

Rescue Brigadesman, Frank Ramsay, is second left here, with Bill Burfield, George Fulthorpe and Jack Evans. They were attending an explosion at Choppington Pit in Northumberland in 1948 which claimed the life of Jim Prime, a deputy.

Young lads at Elemore Colliery. On the left is fourteen-year-old James (Jimmy) Crawford and this photograph was taken on his first day at the pit. He worked at Elemore all his life until he was killed at the pit on 1st November 1955. He was Secretary of the Deputies' Union. A local newspaper gave an account of the inquest held after Mr Crawford's death, one of many personal tragedies of the Durham Coalfield:

'A deputy found dead in Elemore Colliery on 1st November was found on examination to have a fractured spine and bruises on the body, a Hetton inquest was told on Wednesday.

The Coroner, Mr T.V. Devey, sitting with a jury, found that James Crawford (49), James Terrace, Easington Lane, died accidentally after being caught between a set of moving tubs and an overhead conveyer belt. Evidence of identification was given by the widow, Mrs Lily Crawford.

John Goundry, a driller, Grassmere Avenue, Easington Lane, said he went to the meeting place in the South District of the Harvey Seam at 7.50 am. Later he went inbye and at 8.15 am found Crawford lying on the floor between the tub track and the conveyor belt. His head was pointing inbye and his waistcoat was dragged over his head and lying on his hands. Crawford's body was lying about 15 yards on the outbye side of the leading tubs under the conveyor belt. His cap-lamp belt, stick and safety lamp were scattered at different distances.

Replying to Mr J.U.C. Chester, Inspector of Mines, Goundry agreed that the position of these and the body seemed to suggest that Crawford had crossed between the tubs as they were moving and might have been trapped between the top of one of the tubs and the under side of the belt.

John H. Iley, North Street, East Rainton, a deputy overman, said he picked up Crawford's belt with cap-lamp attached. The belt had snapped clean at the back opposite the fastener. He also agreed with Mr Chester's suggestion that Crawford may have been caught between the conveyor belt and tubs while trying to cross at the Fourth East Conveyor and carried forward to where his body was found.

In his summing-up Mr Devey said it seemed obvious that Crawford had been caught up by something and carried for some distance. In his opinion the man had died through being caught between the tub and the belt.

He expressed sympathy with Mrs Crawford, and Mr J.U.C. Chester and Mr R. Kinghorn (NCB) associated themselves with his sentiments.'

Mines' Rescue

An early history of the Rescue Service was given in a brochure produced by the Brigade:

'In 1910 a Rescue Committee was formed by the Durham and Northumberland Coal Owners' Association under the Chairmanship of Colonel W.C. Blackett, and a Rescue Station was erected at Elswick, Newcastle-upon-Tyne.

Mr Guy Symond (now Fire Adviser to the Home Office), then Chief Officer of the Works Fire Brigade of Sir W.G. Armstrong Whitworth & Co Ltd, was appointed in charge of the Brigade with a permanent staff of men.

Recognising early that fire would probably require more serious consideration than would be the results of explosions, the colliery owners determined not only to have men trained in the use of breathing apparatus, but also to have them skilled to fight fires.

A motor engine and a motor rescue tender were provided and equipped for emergencies of fire and explosion at mines.

A Durham & Northumberland Colliery Fire & Rescue Brigade Badge.

In 1911 the Coal Mines' Act was passed with Regulations which made it the duty of the Coal Owners to make adequate provision for the establishment of Central Rescue Stations and for the maintenance of rescue appliances within every 10 miles radius of coal mines.

The organisation was extended, and Central Rescue Stations were erected at Ashington, Northumberland, Houghton-le-Spring and Crook, Co Durham.

These were equipped with motor fire engines and rescue cars, appliances, and a permanent staff of men at each.

Since 1913 the Brigade has been under the charge of Mr F.P. Mills, and with an enthusiastic committee has continued to maintain the Brigade up to modern standards.'

Fire and Rescue Engines at Houghton-le-Spring in 1914, a year after it was opened. To the right are the houses for the rescue workers stationed there.

Rescue teams at Crook. The building is now used by pigeon fanciers to store their transporters and other equipment.

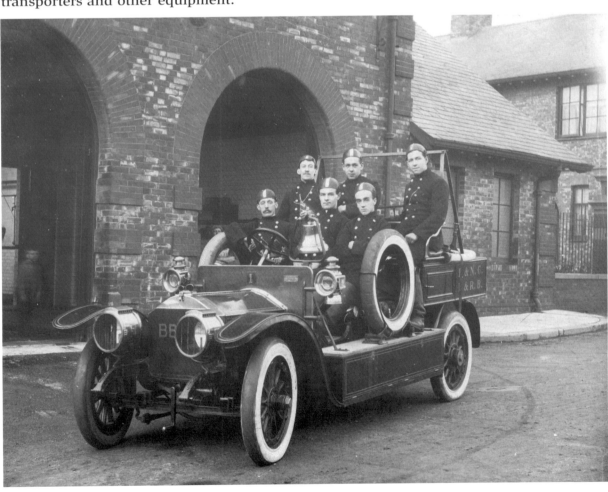

A team with Meco breathing apparatus at South Moor Rescue Station. After the Mines' Accident (Rescue & Aid) Act came into force in 1912, Meco – Mining Engineering Company Ltd based in Sheffield – received inquiries for 500 rescue apparatus sets. A foreman at Meco, Henry Hall, was awarded the OBE for his work with reviving apparatus during the First World War. He carried out his work at their isolated explosive factory near Gretna Green. The rescue apparatus business was sold to Siebe Gorman & Co in 1925 who relocated to Worcester. They later became well known throughout the mining industry for their Meco-Moore leather loaders and conveyors.

Washington, Elemore and Hetton Collieries Rescue team, 1919.

Men with breathing rescue apparatus probably in the Shildon area. The postcard was photographed by Smithson of Shildon.

Prize winners at Houghton-le-Spring Rescue Station in October 1989. Left to right, Bob Grey, Steve Sutherland, Barry Graham, Steve Tiplady and David Hardy. They were winners of the Sir Richard Pease Trophy – the Senior Miners' First Aid Competition. All of them were permanent Brigade men who lived in the nearby tied cottages. They were dedicated men who were picked for their high qualities. The Houghton Station is still operating today, covering Ellington and other smaller mines in the area as well as providing training.

SECTION FIVE

LOOKING AFTER ONE ANOTHER

The visit of representatives of subscribing collieries and works to the Durham County Hospital Convalescent Home, Harrogate, 17th August 1912. Now demolised, the building was next to the Royal Bath Hospital and Valley Gardens.

Conishead Priory Convalescent Home For Durham Mine Workers, 1930-69
by Dorothy A. Rand

An aerial view of Conishead Priory, Convalescent Home for Durham Miners. This postcard from Bertie in 1932 reads: 'This I think, is the best picture, in the card line, to convey what our Convalescent Home is like and its beautiful surroundings. Monday and Tuesday thought I wouldn't manage, now feel sure I can carry on, and get improved somewhat.'

A postcard sent from Ulverston to Waldridge Fell, Chester-le-Street. The message reads: 'Arrived safe, grand place, too long a ride – George.'

112

A composite view of Conishead Priory. Durham County Miners' Welfare Committee wished to find suitable premises for use as a convalescent home. Following the breakdown of negotiations for the purchase of Hexham Hydro in 1928 they were made aware that Conishead Priory, which had been for some years a hydropathic establishment, was for sale. It was a beautiful property, well equipped and in the centre of a large and well wooded estate. It was an ideal place for convalescence, on the coast of Morecambe Bay, sheltered and amid beautiful scenery.

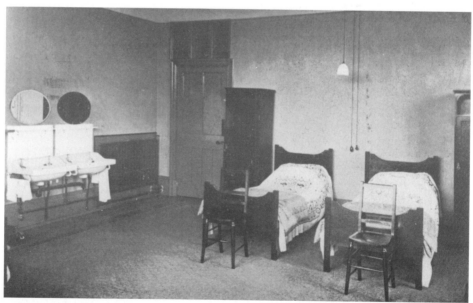

W.A. Kellett, a prominent County Durham architect submitted plans for alterations. The bedrooms were furnished through the Co-operative Wholesale Society with up-to-date furniture made in their own works. Each bedroom had hot and cold water, there were bathrooms on each floor, and there were also Turkish baths and spray baths of hot and cold sea water. Central heating was installed and a self actuating electric passenger lift. Land was available for cattle and poultry to give a supply of fresh food. In 1930 the committee invested £235,000 in various stocks to bring in an annual revenue of over £10,000 for the upkeep of the home.

This Tablet commemorates
the Opening Ceremony of the
Convalescent Home.

The home was opened on 23rd August 1930 by Alderman Thomas Taylor JP, Chairman of the Durham Coal Owners' Association and James Robson JP, President of the Durham Miners' Association. Miners who wished to spend a week (this was later extended to a fortnight) at Conishead applied to the Lodge Secretary, names were chosen by ballot. Applications were often made following injury or illness.

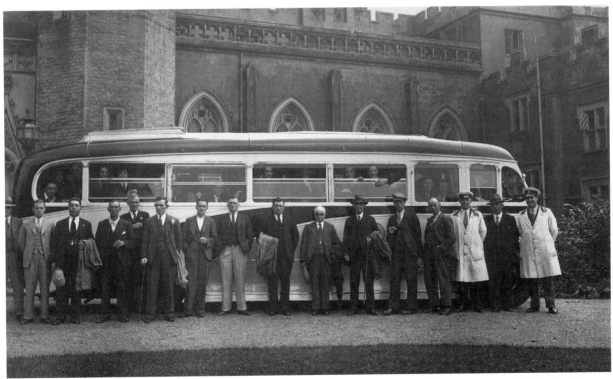

Teddy Calland, a colliery joiner from East Hedley Hope, had almost severed his foot with an adze. He is seventh from the right on this photograph. At first the miners travelled to Conishead by train, but in later years, as the railways dwindled, they were taken by bus. Great emphasis was placed on good food, rest and recreation.

Oak Room, Conishead Priory.   07429 J.V.

The beautiful Oak Room and the Library could be used, and a supply of headed notepaper was available for letters home. Many preferred to send the postcards specially produced and the messages are interesting to read:

'I go to bed at ten and get up at seven when the bell rings and breakfast is at half past eight. It is nice being here, plenty rooms to go in over the fires. When I want a bit lay down on the couch I take the rug over and have a good sleep. There is about a hundred and fifty in this time, a good few short.'

'You will not know me when I come home, I am like a big brewer just eating and drinking.'

Other messages tell of good food and 'its a great place'.

115

Souvenir photographs were taken at Conishead Priory.

Left: My grandfather, John William Spurr, is front right, wearing a silver watch chain made up of a medallion and bars awarded by St John Ambulance Brigade for proficiency in First Aid.

Below: He is seen again, second left, in the back row of this typical group photograph.

Souvenir pottery was also produced, Crown Devon made cups and saucers, plates and beakers in distinctive orange lustre with a drawing of Conishead Priory and the legend: 'Happy Memories Conishead Priory'.

A group posed in 1939. Note the sandbags by the door. During the Second World War Conishead Priory was used as a Military Hospital then returned to the Durham Miners until closure in December 1969. The home featured in an article in the *Durham Advertiser* in September 1952:

'Conishead Priory provides health and recreation of mind and body for some 2,800 men each year. As the present matron says: "Only the best and the very best is good enough for this happy breed of men." And so it is. The Priory is their retreat, their interlude from the grim job they daily undertake. Pride of possession is plainly seen in their faces, their approach and their demeanour. And individual forgetfulness or excess evokes from the men themselves the sternest rebuke. Many are the occasions I join the groups in the corridor or cloisters and listen. I find a variety of subjects are intelligently discussed ranging from racing to religion, politics to pigeons, sport to sociology.'

The miners' pride of possession is reflected in the choice of Conishead Priory as a subject on many colliery banners.

Following closure, Conishead Priory was bought by Buddhists in 1976. One hundred out of the one hundred and seventy acres of grounds were sold to raise money for careful restoration of the building, badly affected by dry rot. By 1995 £900,000 had been spent on restoration including Christian features such as the stained glass windows. A Temple was built in the walled gardens, the bowling green is now a green area and the lake is still there. This Buddhist Residential College is a Manjushri Mahayana Buddhist Centre with about a hundred residents including twenty ordained monks and nuns. It is possible to visit the premises at certain times. Founded in 1160 by Augustinian monks as a hospital for the poor, Conishead Priory now has different monks who look after people's minds.

Aged Miners' Homes

Homes for Aged Miners presented by Mrs Joicey to the Miners' Institute, Pelton. A postcard sent in 1908. Durham Aged Miners' Homes Association was founded in 1898 by Joseph Hopper from Sheriff Hill, Gateshead. The book *A Century Of Care* describes the Association's early days:

'It is not difficult to find Aged Miners' Homes in County Durham – they are present in over 70 villages. This did not happen by chance, but grew from the vision of Joseph Hopper, a miner and lay preacher, who believed that a man who had served in the coalmines from the age of 12 to 65 or beyond deserved better than to be evicted from his tied colliery home when he retired.'

Today the Association manages over 1,400 self-contained homes where residents enjoy affordable rents with caring and responsible staff providing an excellent service.

The opening ceremony of the Aged Miners' Homes at Langley Park on 5th July 1924.

Residents of Aged Miners' Homes at Brandon.

George L. Atkinson in his book, *The Miners' Heritage – A History Of The Durham Mineworkers' Association*, gives a list of rules for the Joicey Aged Miners' Homes:

This house is permitted to be occupied by the tenant at the will of the Lambton Collieries Limited, subject to the following rules:

1. The tenant must be of sober, respectable habits, and must not be guilty of or permit any disorderly conduct.

2. The tenant must cultivate and keep in good order the front garden.

3. The tenant must not keep lodgers but will be allowed to have visitors for a short period of time only.

4. The tenant, being given reasonable notice by the Lambton Collieries Limited, or their agents, shall in a peaceable manner give up vacant possession.

5. The tenant will be supplied with sufficient fire coal for domestic use in the house only.

6. If the tenant dies and leaves a widow of less than 55 years she will be required to vacate the house on being given reasonable notice.

7. If any fittings, blinds, curtains, window panes, &c., shall need repair, the tenant shall report the same without delay to the House Inspector of the Lambton Collieries Limited.

Horden Ambulance Garage and Driver's Cottage in the 1930s. The garage was large enough to accommodate two ambulances. The cottage had a living room, kitchen and scullery, three bedrooms and a bathroom. Schemes such as this were funded, in the these pre-Welfare State days, by the Welfare Funds set up after the 1920 Factories Act which ordered employers to provide amenities for their workers.

One more unusual scheme from the 1930s was described in a 'Welfare Magazine':

'An interesting scheme promoted by the Durham District Committee is that for providing invalid chairs. A total of £1,027, including

£189 in 1937, has been granted for this purpose which comes under the heading of Special Medical Treatment and Appliances. In 1936, there were 14 schemes in operation with a total of 29 chairs, of which 8 were motor-driven, 14 were hand-propelled, 6 were spinal chairs and 1 was a chair for indoor use; 15 of the chairs had been in constant use during the year and 9 had been in intermittent use.'

An ambulance for the British Red Cross Society and St John Ambulance presented by the Durham Miners' Association.

First Aid And The Miner
by Winifred M. Gray

In the early part of the 19th century provision for treatment of injured miners was poor and it was not until 1877 that The Order of St John of Jerusalem formed the St John Ambulance Association in order to teach First Aid and to distribute material to areas where the risks of accidents were high. This was followed in 1877 by the formation of the St John Ambulance Brigade, which enabled people trained in First Aid to practice their skills for the benefit of others. The St John Ambulance Brigade in Durham was largely formed from mining communities; nearly every colliery village had its Ambulance Division.

In 1887, an Ambulance Crusade took place throughout the Counties of Northumberland and Durham where the new Mines' Regulations Act was explained. It related to the provision of stretchers in collieries; instruction of miners in First Aid and the transport of the injured. The first Public Review of First Aiders of any size with demonstration of ambulance work was held at Beamish Park. As many as 310 men from twenty-six collieries within a radius of six miles, all wearing the badge of the Association took part in the parade. The programme included an 'exhibition' of individuals supposed injured because of a mine explosion.

Members of St John who gained the First Aid Certificate and continued successfully for three years qualified for the issue of a Medallion which had the member's name and number inscribed on the reverse side. If he continued to requalify each year, he was awarded a bar to the Medallion bearing the year of issue and the person's number. Many proudly wore the Medallion and bars in the form of watch chains, which made them easily recognisable as 'First Aiders'.

In 1910, the Mines' Rescue & Aid Act required that competent Rescue Brigades be organised and maintained in mines. Each member had to hold the First Aid certificate of St John or the St Andrew's Association. Further impetus was given to the work of the St John Ambulance Association under the provision of the Mines' Accident (Rescue And Aid) Act 1910, where it was ordered that the Mines' Rescue Brigades should be proportionate to the number of underground employees. The rescue brigades had to consist of five people, certified medically fit and qualified to render First Aid through possession of the certificate of the St John Ambulance Association; the St Andrew's Association or other recognised safety. Candidates for manager and under-manager of coal mines had also to be qualified in First Aid.

Murton St John Ambulance Brigade. Back row: Sergeant J.R. Sainty, T. Holland, J. Stokoe, Corporal W. Salkeld, J. Every, W.H. Wilson. Front row: Geo Watkin, E. Seymour Wood, Dr W.H. Gaunt.

First Aid Training And Competitions

First Aid Competitions were informally instituted in 1893 and conducted at the Annual Camps of Instruction by the St John Ambulance Brigade. The gift of a shield, now known as the 'Dewar Shield' from Sir Thomas Dewar, Sheriff of London 'to commemorate the Diamond Jubilee of Queen Victoria and for competition among the Divisions of the Brigade.' The shield became the principal award at the Brigade's Competition and was first won by a Durham team – Murton Colliery – in 1912. The Dean & Chapter Colliery team in 1959, then Dawdon Colliery followed this in 1974 and 1981.

In 1904 Mr Donald Bain, a Senior HM Inspector of Mines in Durham, presented a shield for competition between teams of men employed in mines (including lead and ironstone). In the first year teams consisted of eight members, this was changed the following year to five. It was not uncommon for sixty teams to enter the contest; the final was always held in the Durham Town Hall. The first team to win the trophy was Murton Colliery. Teams in the 1948 final included: Blackhall Colliery, Chilton Colliery, Dean & Chapter Colliery, Horden Colliery and North Skelton Ironstone Mine. Later in 1925, a Junior Competition was introduced, Mrs Elizabeth Bain, the wife of Mr Donald Bain, presented a shield which bears her name.

Mr John Graham DL, a Coroner for the Chester Ward in Durham expressed concern at the number of inquests involving miners. In order to encourage training he presented a shield to St John Ambulance in Durham for annual competition. The first contest was held in 1926 with 30 teams in the preliminary rounds. The proprietors of the *North Mail* provided a shield for the team gaining second place. The finals were again held in the Durham Town Hall. The six teams competing in the first final were Brandon Colliery, Tyne Dock LNER, Dean & Chapter Colliery, Gateshead Police, Blackhall Colliery and Boldon Colliery.

Dean and Chapter St John Ambulance Brigade in the 1950s. Team members at that time included: Billy Wright, Billy McAdam (Captain), Lance Smith, George Kerry, Ralph Gibson and J. Kellet.

The prize winning Dawdon St John Ambulance Brigade. Standing, left to right: I.B. Storey, George Bowerbank, Jimmy Peacock, Jimmy Dickinson, John Fletcher and Bobby Milford. Seated: Kenny Henderson (Colliery Manager) and Ralph Sanderson (Deputy Manager). George Bowerbank has recently compiled two books listing the teams, team members and scenarios for those who competed in the NCB and British Coal National First Aid Competition Finals from 1949 to 1994. They illustrate the importance that First Aid played in the life of the miner.

The National Coal Board followed the pattern of most National Industries and held its own National First Aid Competition for both Senior and Junior Teams. In 1949, the Donald Bain Shield was presented to the Durham Division for annual competition; the winning team would represent the region at the National Final. The interest in competitions throughout the mining industry was intense and teams from Durham often appeared in the top three places in the national competition.

In 1955, Deaf Hill Colliery won the Junior Section of the National Coal Board's First Aid Competition. A year later the Shotton Colliery team won the Senior Section and received the Mitchel Hedges Trophy which was 31in high, 37in long and weighed 97lbs. Further success was achieved in 1958 when the Dean & Chapter Colliery won both the Senior and Junior Trophies and in 1959 the coveted Grand Prior's Trophy.

Because of the inherent dangers within the mining industry, it is readily understood why miners practised First Aid so enthusiastically. Most collieries had at least one First Aid Team and many of their names appear not only on trophies within Durham but on National trophies. Despite the demise of the coal industry, First Aid Competition work continues within the County of Durham and many ex-miners are training a new generation of competitors.

A Friend In Need
by Dorothy A. Rand

There are many stories of courage in the mines, this one involves two members of the Burnopfield Division of St John Ambulance Brigade. In 1966 Charlie Metcalf was awarded the St John Life Saving Medal – the first in County Durham – for risking his life to help his friend and colleague, Billy McKie. Billy remembers going down Byermoor Pit at 8.00 am. At 8.10 he was buried in a serious fall of stone by the collapse of the old haulage house at the shaft bottom.

Two other men were brought out but Billy was trapped for two hours under the debris with a broken arm, head injuries and many broken ribs. The Colliery Medical Attendant was Charlie Metcalf who was also Superintendent of the Burnopfield Division of St John Ambulance Brigade. He crawled through the debris to give much-needed morphine then more stones fell and the rescuers pulled Charlie out by his feet. Billy felt that his chest was going to burst and asked for a second dose of morphine. Charlie risked his life to do this, shaking off rescuers who tried to pull him back.

The next thing Billy remembers was the sunshine when he was brought to the surface. He recalls:

As the road to the shaft bottom was closed the workers had to carry me through the airway to the upcast shaft. I understand this was organised by some top brass from the Area. I was told it was marvellous how he arranged for different workers to change over to carry the stretcher.

The next thing I remember was being in a hospital bed and two nurses were draining my lungs. I heard one say, "Thank goodness he doesn't smoke." When I got home I told my doctor of this and he said, "If you were a smoker you would not have lived." I understand that I was not washed for several days. As I was on a breathing machine and could not talk and my right arm was broken I had difficulty in telling anyone anything. Jean, my wife, brought me a notepad and pen in and I tried to write with my left hand.

There was a time when I was too frightened to go to sleep because of nightmares. I was in a prisoner-of-war camp attached by a wire through my neck and I was running along with all the other prisoners attached by a wire. I found it difficult to tell a nurse so I managed to write a note explaining about my dreams. The doctor decided to stop the injections and give me tablets instead, so they sat me up and I passed out. The next memory is of a team of doctors and machines around me. The consultant, Mr Petty, came, he rubbed the top of my head and said, "You're a tough little miner!" After two weeks they sent me to Holywood Hall (formerly Wolsingham Sanatorium) to convalesce.

Byermoor Colliery.

I was off work for six months then back down the pit on my own job (colliery overman) but after a couple of weeks I had a little breakdown so I was given a job on the surface for a few weeks. But I was soon back down and stayed until the pit closed in 1968. I was the last one out of the pit, I was in charge at the end. Just before I came up in the cage I picked a piece of coal up, this was the last coal from Byermoor and it is now in my garage. After I came to the surface that day we took the cages off. So ended the life of a coal mine.

When the colliery was closed a reporter from the local paper came to see the manager. In conversation, the reporter said he came from Australia. When he asked the manager, "How long has there been a colliery at Byermoor?"

He replied, "Byermoor Colliery was here before they discovered your country!"

Billy obtained his First Aid Certificate in 1938 aged 21, he had his Deputy's Certificate at the age of 22 although not able to do deputy's work until 25. After a short time as deputy he was appointed overman then, in later years, material controller. He stayed on with St John Ambulance Brigade and gave much of his time, particularly in the training of cadets. He became a Serving Brother and ten years later when Tyne and Wear was created, and he had to transfer to Northumbria, Dr Burns nominated him to become Officer Brother as a thank you for all the work he had done for St John Ambulance in County Durham. Now 84, Billy is still working enthusiastically for the organisation as Secretary of the Gateshead branch of the St John Fellowship.

Billy McKie shares a joke while being made an Officer Brother of St John Ambulance at St John's Gate in London.

Byermoor Colliery First Aid Team. Back row, right to left: C. Metcalf, W. McKie, E. Gibson, J. Bainbridge and A. Robson. Front row: Major Nicholson, Sir Myers Wayman and C. Mills.

Billy McKie is second from the left in the row of people administering artificial respiration at Hobson Colliery during the Second World War, when extra surface workers were trained in First Aid and Rescue Work. The post was manned every night at first, but later only when the Air Raid alarm sounded. 'If the raid lasted two hours we got a chocolate biscuit, if it only lasted one hour 59 minutes we got nothing. I still remember those chocolate biscuits.' Billy recalls that the standard of First Aid in the mines was very good, mainly due to First Aid Competitions and Rescue Training at the collieries, Byermoor had a very keen team and Billy has many medals to mark their success.

Hobson Colliery.

THE BIG MEETING

Usworth Lodge Banner at the Gala around 1970.

Outside the Swan Inn, Waldridge Fell, locals are about to leave for the Gala, around 1910. All that remains today is the Waldridge Tavern on the right. The Square has been demolished.

South Pelaw Colliery band and banner at Durham on Big Meeting Day.

A Day To Remember

Living in a colliery house, and growing up in a pit village in County Durham in the 1950s, brings vivid memories of some hard times. Throughout, these sometimes cold and hungry years, there were always days of sunshine, and it is these days that seem to last longer in the memory.

One such day was Christmas Day which was always waited for in eager anticipation. The few but treasured Christmas presents and the abundance of sweets, nuts and fruit made life feel good.

Another such day was that of the Big Meeting at Durham, it was so important to mining families throughout the county. Some weeks before the meeting miners would gather to select the men to carry the banner and its associated ropes with tassels. This period was the start of the excitement, knowing Durham Day was not far off. It was indeed an honour and a privilege to be selected to represent the lodge by carrying the banner and it made the whole family very proud.

Durham Day started early in our house, we quickly got dressed and washed and gulped our breakfast of porridge, before running the messages up the shop for bread and cigarettes, after which you could go out and play.

Most of the kids from the colliery houses made their way up to the Workingmen's Club, to wait outside and watch whilst the men with the banner were readied. They all formed a column with the bandmaster leading and the banner lined up behind the

Hylton Colliery Silver Band and various members of the Miners' Union, outside the Castletown Welfare Hall around 1955.

Hylton Colliery Silver Band was formed in 1949 and disbanded in 1979. The band are standing, left to right: Herbert Cope, unknown, Jim Taylor, Jimmy Brownless, Robert Taylor, Chris Surtees, Leslie Bell, John Haley, Dennis Brownless, Ray Reid, W. Archibald, Tommy Burgess, Jim Elland, Jimmy Farrel, W. Archibald Jnr, Bill Baharie, Bill Craggs, Teddy Ward, George Graham, Gilbert Crossley, Ron Snowdon, Jimmy McDermitt, Maurice Woodmas and John Graham. Seated, left to right: Teddy Walton, George Cope, Jimmy Anderson, James Wood, George Scott, Harry Brown, Harry Graham, George Vickers, Tommy Golightly, J. O'Neil, Councillor Bowmaker, George Scott, George Clarke, Walter Wilson and James Brownless.

Burnhope Lodge Banner, Band and followers about to set off for the Gala.

band. While the column moved off, miners and their families joined in by lining-up behind their banner.

The procession would march through the village, up the main road, passing the shops and the crowds of people gathered on the corner end of the rows of colliery houses. The villagers would cheer and clap as the procession passed them. Throughout the parade, children would follow alongside, skipping and jumping excitedly and pointing out their friends in the column.

The abiding memory of the procession, was the shiver down your back and the hair on the back of your neck standing on end when the band was playing. The whole event made everyone very happy and proud of the village and its pit. The parade was stopped at the cricket ground and the band, union men, the miners and their families would pile into the waiting 'trip buses' and all were quickly away to Durham, and it was still just after 7 o'clock in the morning.

During the day the village was like a ghost town. The children left behind would gather to play and the main topic of conversation was, 'When are you going to join the band?' The adults left seemed to be discussing whether or not our band was first into Durham. In those days there was a great sense of belonging, in being part of a mining community and family life was at its most recognisable with Mam always there whenever you needed her. The day soon passed and as it neared 5 o'clock the kids would make their way up to the cricket field to await the buses return from Durham.

When the buses arrived back, the band and the banner would assemble outside the cricket ground. These would be proceeded by a line of boys and girls, mams and dads dressed in cowboy hats and 'Kiss Me Quick' hats. This line would stretch right across the road from side to side with all their arms linked behind their backs. As soon as the band struck-up, the front line began singing and yelling with joy and happiness. As the procession moved off down the road, the line swayed from side to side and they danced and sang to the music of the band. It was obvious some of the front line revellers were the worse for wear after the long day at Durham on the beer. The line would meander across the road sometimes colliding with the lampposts or people gathered along the roadside, it would also regularly collapse but the line would soon be reformed and continue on, merrily all the way through the village.

As the procession moved down through the village, the band would play some rousing music, much to the delight of the villagers who clapped and cheered and shouted good wishes to all in the parade. Some of the bandsmen had their hats tilted to one side and their lines wavered slightly. Throughout all the proceedings the big drum kept that regular beat (with or without music) and kept everyone in step. The miners holding the banner and its ropes could be seen to wander violently from side to side, the swing being directly attributable to the amount of alcohol consumed during the day.

The procession stopped outside the Workingmen's Club where it had started earlier in the day. After forming a semi-circle around the banner, which was rested against the wall of the club, the band would play the last tune. This tune would be some poignant lament dedicated to the memory of all miners who had lost their lives in the mining industry.

Invariably, with the music over, all bandsmen and banner men dispersed, some into the club, others were taken home by their families giving them some welcome support. The talk at home was of the events of the day at Durham, and the distribution of presents like candy rock and novelties for the younger children of the family and sometimes a present for Mam.

Those days have now faded into the past but will always be fondly remembered. It is important to recall the contribution village life, the pit, the band, and the unions made in the formative years of recent generations, it made us the people we are today.

It did not matter that you did not get to Durham, there was always next year to look forward to.

Ouston 'E' Lodge Banner outside the Coach and Horses, Birtley.

Big Meeting Day
by Jack Hair

My dad worked at East Tanfield and the biggest event of the year was the Durham Miners' Gala held in Durham City. Each colliery had its own miners' lodge affiliated to the DMA.

At the local meeting of each lodge, they would draw out the names of those men selected to carry the banner into Durham. There would be two men on the poles and four on the banner strings. Six men would carry the banner in and out of Durham. Only fully paid-up union members were allowed to carry the banner.

Some collieries like Craghead, South Moor and the Morrison and others had their own brass bands. Others would hire a band in for the day. It was the custom for most collieries to parade in their own villages before travelling into Durham. Several of the local Stanley pits would march either up or down Stanley Street before they made their trip into Durham. East Tanfield used to meet at the Empire Club, Stanley. Because it was a special day, drinks were allowed. The band were always sent over to the Co-op Cafe for their early morning breakfast and then it was time to go. Buses had been hired in for the men and their families. Once in Durham our assembly point was the Garden House pub. The brightly painted banner was taken out of its bag and placed over the poles. The men lined up. The band first, followed by the banner and officials and behind the banner were the miners and their families. The banner was a symbol of that particular lodge and there was a great feeling of pride and affiliation to your pit and banner swelling up inside you.

The scene as you went down under the railway arches was staggering. There, waiting, were tens of thousands of people lining the streets, all the way down to the bridge at the bottom of Silver Street. Up above were the Castle and Cathedral, and even these went unseen amidst this grand spectacle.

On one such day, as we reached the bottom of Silver Street, everything came to a halt as the bands ahead were unable to move any further. These narrow streets were filled to capacity with not a spare inch to move. The bands were still playing and the crowds still singing and the different tunes ran into each other until it was difficult to separate one from the other.

Slowly, we struggled up this street before turning to go down to Elvet and see the politicians of the day on the balcony of the County Hotel. At this point the crowds were like a sea of people, no beginning and no end. With the politicians were other dignitaries and invited guests. Some bands would stop there and play a special tune thus holding up the following bands and banners.

The banner of Chester Moor Colliery parades through Durham on Gala day.

Blackhall Lodge Banner on Elvet Bridge in the 1950s.

Ryhope Lodge Banner at the Gala in the 1950s.

Eventually we reached the top of the bank leading down to the Sands Racecourse. This view was also spectacular. The whole area seemed covered with people, bands and banners. It was possible to hear at least ten bands before you and as many following on.

Once we reached our designated area, the banner was set down against a fence and the band instruments placed in front of it. The banner carriers could at last take off their carrying straps and have a well earned rest. Many would go off to the nearest pub, while others sat where they could for a meal with their families and friends. During the afternoon, the remainder of the lodges and their banners continued to make their way down to the racecourse. Many people went down to the riverside to have a row on the boats. Meanwhile the politicians gave their speeches from the raised platform and could be heard all over through the loud speakers dotted around the course.

Many of the fairground shows that had been to Newcastle Races had made the journey to the Gala and a good time was had by all. One of the years that my dad carried the banner, Mam had bought him a new white shirt for the occasion. With temperatures soaring and the task of carrying the banner, he sweated profusely. This was still the days of the tin bath and the sweat brought out the coal dust from his pores and his new shirt was stained in coal dust sweat. He was so proud of carrying this banner.

Some of the banners and lodges had been up to the Cathedral for a service. By the time the last lodge came down on to the Course, it was virtually time for the first to have arrived to lift the banner and head back up the steep ramp to head back through the city. Some of the banners were edged in black. This signified there had been a death or deaths in that colliery. Once, Easington Banner was almost totally draped in black due to the disaster there in October 1953 when 83 miners lost their lives.

The journey out was even livelier due to the merriment and drink during the day. Many of the younger people would link arms almost the width of the road and dance side to side down through the narrow streets. It was a time of celebration. I know how

Washington 'F' Pit Lodge Banner leaving Durham Cathedral.

Easington Lodge Banner, draped in black.

The parade passes the Three Tuns Hotel in New Elvet on a rainy day in the mid 1960s.

proud I felt, walking just near my dad, in the shadow of the banner that he was carrying. He and his colleagues represented their lodge, their pit and their town with great pride and dignity. In 1949 they had won the Production Banner, the first ever awarded, and Dad was drawn to carry this banner.

Eventually the bands would reach the area near Dryburn Hospital where the buses were waiting for them to return home. On arrival at Stanley the banner would be unfurled once more. The banner men would again raise it to the sky and, following the band, would march up Stanley Street amidst great cheers from local people. A grand day!

Many years previously my Grandfather Hair, also a miner, had been to the Gala. He didn't normally drink but that day was an exception. On arriving home, some men came to my gran's house and asked her for the piano. Apparently, while at Durham, he had sold it to some of his friends and had failed to tell her.

One of the best bands I ever heard at Durham was in 1960 when Tanfield Lea Colliery engaged the 751 United States Air Force Band. This band was a marching and counter marching band and even counter marched on parade while still playing. They too, played in Stanley before going off to Durham where they had a rapturous welcome. The people of Tanfield Lea definitely danced in and out of Durham that day. American Ambassador, J.H. Witney, attended that meeting at Durham and forecast the winner of a horse race later that day – and it won!

The band also gave a performance for the local people over that weekend at Murray Park, Stanley. Long gone are those heady days, even though there is still a so-called Miners' Gala. Though still popular, it has lost some of its meaning now that the coal mines no longer exist and the miners no longer employed. All that's really left are the memories. This is not intended to denigrate the small mines which still exist. I talk mostly of the years of the deep mining industry. Many young adults can't even remember coal mines in our area. Long gone are the pitheads and pit heaps. The area has reverted back to countryside.

The Vane Tempest Lodge Banner and supporters march down New Elvet.

Harraton Lodge Banner in Durham in the mid 1960s.

Washington
Glebe Lodge
Banner in
the 1970s.

A baton twirler leads the way on the corner of New Elvet and Old Elvet during the Gala in the late 1960s.

The Hylton Lodge Banner heading down to Elvet Bridge.

Miners' leader and MP, Jack Lawson, describes the Gala just before the Second World War in his book, *A Man's Life*:

'It is exhilarating to march with your band and banner, and also to watch this stirring spectacle from some high point of vantage where you see it as a continuous whole. Officially this gathering is called a gala, but to miners and their wives, who come in from every part of Durham, it is 'The Big Meeting'. Banner after banner, band after band, followed by members of the Lodges and their wives. From remote places on moor and fell, and from huge collieries near the towns, they have marched; down from the boundaries of the coalfield, and up from the centre they have come keeping step all along the roads to lively tunes. Since eight in the morning they have been coming into the city of Durham, and even at noon the apparently endless march goes on. First comes the great banner carried by picked men, who must know how to carry themselves, or their strength will avail them little. Poising the poles in the brass cup resting on the chest, and held by leather straps on the shoulders, is a great art ...

The officials of the Lodge walk with pride beneath their banner, while behind comes the band and the men and women of the colliery. Down the main street they walk, between walls of spectators massed together on either side. Greetings are called by the onlookers to friends and relatives in the procession, and hands are gripped as they pass on. Sometimes the march is slowed down, sometimes it is stopped, marches and spectators blocking the long street as far as eye can see.'

A Chelsea Pensioner leads the way for the Mainsforth Lodge Banner at the Gala in the 1950s.

Deaf Hill Lodge Banner – showing Conishead Priory – on Elvet Bridge in the 1950s.

The Roddymoor Lodge Banner passes the old County Hall in Old Elvet, with the castle in the background.

Crowds on the racecourse on Big Meeting Day in the 1950s.

Clem Attlee and Sam Watson make their way through the crowd at the racecourse.

This photograph gives a vivid impression of what Big Meeting Day was like in its heyday. The crowds pack the area in front of the Royal County Hotel.

The Gala in the early 1970s with a group of youngsters dancing arm in arm.

The Banner
by Derek Gillum

The Lodge Banner is one of the lasting symbols of the Durham Coalfield. In 1872 Banners would cost around £24 – about fifty years later that had risen to £43. There was a banner maker in Sunderland, E.D Nichol & Co, and in South Shields, S.M. Peacock.

Most of the Durham banners were made by Tuthills of London. Tuthill, a Yorkshireman, started his business in 1837. Later Turtle and Pearce took over the company.

Although today banners are treasured items of mining history this has not always been the case. Many banners – as their collieries closed – were allowed to be sold, transferred or to deteriorate in poor storage conditions. However, as more and more of our mining heritage was lost, banners regained their place as historic treasures. In 1973 there was a exhibition of twenty Lodge Banners at the Durham Light Infantry Museum – perhaps the first indoor exhibition in the world. Also in the 1970s there were exhibitions of banners at the Miners' Gala.

Today there are numerous funds in former colliery villages to help restore banners to their old homes. The pits may have gone but the banner will live on.

Allerdene Lodge Banner and officials. The banner shows the 'bundle of sticks' fable with the motto 'Unity is strength'.

Jack Lawson in his book, *A Man's Life*, described the importance of the lodge banner:

'The colliery banner is almost a personality. Much thought has been given to colour, design and size. Many have been the consultations with the artist and the firm chosen to carry out the wishes of the Lodge in the matter of bringing this banner to life, and one of the great days in the history of the colliery was the unveiling of it. A colliery without a banner is almost unthinkable. Deep debate on design and finance go to the making of it, and he is an honoured man who is chosen to cut the silken cord and speak to the great crowd which gathers at its unfurling.'

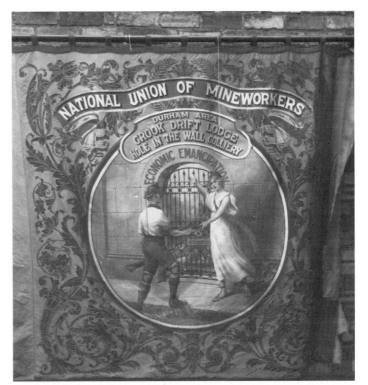

Brandon Lodge Banner. This photograph was taken in Manitoba, Canada. The banner had been given to the City of Brandon in Canada in 1969. Thirty years later the banner returned home and was paraded again at the Gala in 1999. It is now proudly displayed in a specially made case in Brandon (Durham).

Crook Drift Lodge, Hole In The Wall Colliery Banner. A number of drift mines had their own banners.

Below: Marsden Lodge Banner showing the famous Rock – before its recent collapse.

Beamish Air Lodge Banner in the 1950s. This banner – showing a miner and an Australian shaking hands – was replaced in 1959 by a new design of two pitheads and a smoking chimney. Back row, left to right: N. Benfold, R. Muncaster, S. Shield, A. Whittaker, T. Benfold, B. Chapman and J. Dodds. Front row: F. Cornforth (Compensation Secretary), J. Madden (Lodge Chairman), W. Harrison (Treasurer), J. Clark, J. Main (Secretary and Check Weighman) and R. Rowlands. A. Whittaker was the 'average taker' who would ask the men what their take home pay was so he could average it out and inform the union.

AT PLAY

Two quoits players – believed to be from the Ramshaw area.

Harraton Colliery cricket team, 1955. The team are, back row: T. Huscroft, B.F. Humble, A. Dean, W. Charlton and R. Habron. Front row: A. Louth, C. Brown, D. Scott, J. Colpitts, F.G. Swan (colliery manager) and W. King. Also included are: T. Wilson, Hekter, F. Humble (secretary), T. Robinson, F. Grayson, J. Humble (chairman) and T. Robinson (the club's first secretary). At the front is S. Dean (groundsman). The colliery was known locally as the Cotia Pit.

Esh Institute Cricket Club, around 1910.

A Hotbed Of Football

The North East has often been called a 'football hotbed' and this tradition is particularly strong in the colliery communities of County Durham. There have been many great players and teams with strong mining connections.

Murton Colliery Welfare Football Club around 1937. Like many teams in Durham, their home strip was red and white striped shirts with black shorts. In the front row, on the left, is the trainer, James Reed. His wife, Lilian, mended and washed the team's strip and made tea at half time.

In the mid 1930s Murton CW had a very successful side. They won the Monkwearmouth Charity Cup – one of the oldest football competitions in the world – two seasons running, 1934-35 and 1935-36. They were also Wearside League Champions in 1936-37. In the 1930s, the Wearside League was dominated by Colliery Welfare teams. As well as Murton, successful sides included: Blackhall CW, Easington CW, Seaham CW, Horden CW, Lumley Sixth Pit Welfare and Usworth Colliery. Blackhall CW were Wearside League Champions three times in the 1930s and in the 1934-35 season won the Sunderland Shipowners' Cup – one of the most highly contested cups in the North East which was often won by the Reserve sides of Sunderland and Middlesbrough.

After the Second World War, Colliery Welfare sides continued their dominance of local football. Some of the great sides included: South Hetton CW, Shotton CW, Dawdon CW, Boldon CW, Langley Park CW, Silksworth CW and Ryhope CW. Ryhope were a great side in the 1960s winning the Wearside League four times in the decade as well as numerous other trophies. In 1967 they reached the First Round of the FA Cup where they lost 1-0 to Workington Town.

Marsden Colliery Welfare Juniors FC in the mid 1930s. Back row: W, Lister (Secretary), J. Hann, M. Davidson, T. Stephenson, J. Taylor and C. Lister (Trainer). Second row: R. Robinson (Treasurer), R. Dixon, J. Bell (Captain), S. Pearson, and S. Thompson. Front row: R. Stephenson, W. Turner, W. Robinson, W. Bond and H. Hunter. The club was a member of the South Shields Boys' League at the time.

MARSDEN COLLIERY WELFARE JNR. F.C.

Matches between local sides drew great crowds – and celebrities. Here, Eddie Calvert – The Man With The Golden Trumpet – kicks off a match between Easington Lane FC and Eyemouth.

The Aged Miners' Cup and Mid Durham League Cup, won by Wingate Albion AFC in the 1906-07 season, are shown off on the back of this cart.

Chilton Colliery Recreation Athletic FC in the 1930s. Back row: R. Watson, J. Tinkler, F. Gelderd, R. Richardson, H. Dixon, J. Smallwood and G. Whitfield (Trainer). Front row: F. Pickard, M. Palister, W. Alderson, F. Joung and H. Kennedy (Captain). Formed in 1921, the team quickly found success. In the 1923-24 season they reached the semi-final of the Amateur Cup, won the Durham Amateur Cup, Palantine League and Charity Cup. In 1925-26 they won the Northern Alliance and two years later won the Northern League.

Silksworth defenders jump to head off an opposing attack in a Wearside League game on the Welfare pitch in the 1970s. A great day in the history of the club was when they beat Sunderland Reserves 3-0 in the final of the Shipowners' Cup in 1954. A large crowd at the Silksworth Welfare Ground roared them onto victory and there was much celebration in the village after the triumph.

The Mighty Leek
by Neil Taylor

One of the great traditions of the Durham Coalfield is leek growing. Months of hard work leads up to showtime in the pubs, clubs and social centres of the North East. Benching leeks for judging the biggest and best can mean up to two years work for the dedicated showman who develops and grows his own strain. The combination of leeks, veg and flowers gives the showroom a unique aroma like nothing else can. But have you ever wondered how this passion for growing and showing leeks started?

Vying with the pea, chives, onion and garlic as one of the oldest cultivars in existence, it is mentioned in the Bible and dated at least 1500 BC. Of Middle East origin, it was introduced to Britain by the Romans around AD 43. It was noted for its medicinal as well as its culinary uses with the ability to survive the most severe weather.

The emblem of Wales, the leek bears the Cymric colours of green and white – being worn in the hats of Welshmen in battle. It is thought that when St David was a boy, wild leeks grew in the valley where he lived and formed part of his diet.

Leek shows were first held in the North East in the Durham pit villages in the middle of the nineteenth century. Coal owners pursued their sports of shooting, riding and hunting on their estates while the ordinary folk settled for keeping pigeons and growing leeks for the table and then the showbench. The mystique surrounding leek growing came from the growers who jealously guarded their growing and feeding methods. One humorous method used by many was to empty the contents of the kidneys on to the leek bed. This would also be beneficial to the grower, especially if he was passing by the allotments on his way home from the pub.

In the early part of the twentieth century, shops and stores supplied household goods as prizes which attracted interest from the growers' wives. Sadly this practice has ceased and has taken some of the family interest away and much of the gloss from the showhall. During the 1960s and '70s many North East mining families moved to the Midland coalfields with the prospect of housing and secure employment there. The men took with them their leek growing tradition and shows became popular in that region.

The demise of the North East coalfields and its heavy industry, resulting in high unemployment, has seen the closure of many social centres. There has even been the loss of whole communities when villages were demolished and people housed in new estates. All of this means that there are fewer of the smaller shows.

Jack Sewell and Tom Mason with their prize blanch leeks – grown for length and girth – at Waldridge Fell.

However, there is still a cult following of leek growers and especially in Durham and Northumberland – a legacy handed down over the years from father to son. From the 1970s and the formation of the Pot Leek Society, many of the top growers have turned their attention to Open Shows attracting entries from a wide area with big cash prizes. The Farringdon Club in Sunderland,

Easington and Dunston Fed Shows are among these and then there is the World Championship at Ashington

Time has moved on and new cultural methods with improved leek strains has seen the leek brought up to super status with the World Record for three leeks of 6" blanch double that of the 1950s.

The strain of leek is often named after people who produce them or the place from which they originated – such as the Jones, Harry Bone, Sammy Cross, Belsay Blue, Quebec or Thirston to name a few.

Yet there would have been none of these today had it not been for a Roman legionnaire marching in an alien land through wind and rain some 2,000 years ago clutching a handful of wild leek seed with the majestic name of Allium Ampeloprasum. He would have been astounded to see the giant pot leeks grown today. What once started as a pitman's hobby now includes people from all walks of life. From all the many pits in the great Northern Coalfield only Ellington deep mine remains. Yet, the mighty leek lives on.

Two Silksworth men with prize winning leeks in the 1970s.

Prize winners at a Durham City Leek Show in 1956.

Miners from Billy Row, near Crook, with whippet, 'Bayardo', the winner of the Powderhall Handicap in 1911. Back left is Ned Parkin, the 'slipper', and right is Matt Steels, the trainer.

Four Marley Hill miners with their whippets.

Two smart men in front of their even smarter pigeon cree. This postcard was sent from Chester-le-Street to Trimdon Colliery in 1913. The message refers to a pigeon that has not turned up yet. 'It must be a duffer,' the sender wrote.

William Richardson & Son's cree at Ford in Sunderland in 1944. These allotments stood across the river from Hylton Colliery at Castletown. During the Second World War usual pigeon racing had to be suspended because the Germans occupied most of

Bill Richardson and his wife Ethel in front of the loft at Ford. He is holding the Penzance hen.

Bill Richardson

Europe. But some races were still held and Penzance became the farthest race point possible. One of Bill's birds was the only one that homed on the second day of a race from Penzance. However, the race had already been called off when no birds had arrived on the first day and he won nothing. The sire of this bird was given to Jack Curry, a miner at Hylton Colliery, who passed it on to some men who helped form the Castletown pigeon club.

Up North Combine

On the following pages are some images from the Up North Combine – the pigeon fanciers association formed in 1905. They show how a popular pitman's pastime of the nineteenth century has developed into an international sport where pigeon fanciers compete at the highest level.

A group of men with some of the baskets to be loaded on this Bristol Freighter in the late 1950s. There were a total of 202 baskets on this flight.

Unloading a Bristol Freighter at Cormeilles in 1955.

The liberation of birds at Lille in 1958 with French fanciers assisting.

Releasing Up North Combine Birds at Lille in 1961.

Releasing birds at Hitchin in 1946.

The very successful Heydon Brothers of Dawdon holding two of their many trophies.

Messrs Gippert and Henry of New Seaham in the 1950s.

Pigeon racing transporters at Shotton in 1970.

Bands

New Brancepeth Institute Silver Band, outside French's Station Hotel, 1905.

Harton Colliery Band.

Hebburn Colliery Silver Prize Band. They were prize winners at Crystal Palace in 1904.

South Moor Colliery, Silver Prize Band. Winners of the Grand Shield at Crystal Palace in 1907.

St Hilda Colliery Band

One of the most famous bands in the area was the St Hilda Colliery Band who, at Crystal Palace, won the 1,000 Guineas Challenge Trophy in 1912, 1920, 1921, 1924 and 1926. Shortly after the 1926 triumph the band turned professional and toured the country until it was disbanded in 1937.

Bowls, a popular game for young and old. These two ladies are taking part in a game on the men's green in the Welfare Park in Silksworth in the 1970s.

Beamish & East Tanfield Bowling Club, winners of the Shimeld Bowl in 1956.

PIT LIFE

A postcard of School Camp, Blackhall Rock, a typical destination for miners' children. The card was posted to Windemere Street, Gateshead in 1937. The message reads: 'I am enjoying myself immensely down here. Miss Lickfield is my teacher, and we begin lessons tomorrow. I wish you were here as well. I hope you are in the pink again.'

Son of a Coal Miner
by Jack Hair

As the son of a Stanley coal miner, much of my life was centred around the day to day events of the pit. When my dad first left school he wanted to be a builder and worked for some time helping to build houses at the top of Crook Gate Bank Top. At that time he was only 14 years old.

One day, while out shopping with his father (who was a miner at Beamish Mary), the manager of the pit said to Dad's father, 'By, he's a fine big lad. When will he be staring work at the pit?'

His dad said, 'Well he's actually already left school and is working on the building site.'

The pit manager replied quite sharply, 'Bring him to the pit on Monday and if you fail to do so you can look for another job and house.'

Well that was that. My dad reluctantly, but with no other choice, presented himself for work at the pit on the Monday morning.

At that time he was paid 10 shillings a week. Dad was a keen sportsman and played football and cricket for local teams to a high standard. At one time. later on, he could have played League football. He was also a fine athlete. They used to hold athletic meetings on the King's Head Field and, instead of prize money, the prize for winning would be clothing and material vouchers for a local shop. Dad won so many races he virtually clothed all of his family.

When he first married my mother they lived for a while with her parents before getting their colliery house at Middle Street, East Stanley. They had several houses after this, in Joicey Square, Railway Terrace and then eventually to Delacour Street.

Even at home you could not get away from the pit. At different times of the day, various pit hooters would sound off to indicate the pits were working or laid off or for other reasons. Within approximately three miles of our home were many collieries such as: Beamish Air and Mary, the Louisa, Tanfield Lea Margaret, East Tanfield, Morrison North and South and Busty, Shield Row Drift near Quaking Houses, the Hedley Pit, the William Pit, Old South Moor, the Craghead Pits, Burnhope, Hobson, Dipton and others.

SOUTH MOOR. 12309

A typical pit village in the Stanley area – South Moor with the colliery in the foreground.

You could even smell the pit in our kitchen. Mam used to dry Dad's pit clothes in the boiler at the side of the coal fire. He worked in water and the clothes smelt of a type of canker. The smell of these clothes was forever in the houses. When they were dry, Mam would dad (shake) them against the outside wall to remove the dust. In the food pantry, in a tin on the floor, was Dad's supply of Carbide crystals which he used to fuel his Carbide lamp. You would drop a few pieces of Carbide into the lamp and add water. The chemical reaction gave off a gas which then in turn, when ignited, gave off the flame for the light. The lamp had a reflector and once Mam polished it so bright that when Dad went to work the lamp was so bright his marras (workmates) couldn't see for the dazzle.

Marras were a very important part of a miner's life. Quite often your life depended on the man next to you when underground and they shared a great trust in each other. This forged great and lasting friendships away from work.

If you were awake in the early morning you could often hear the sound of the pitmen's boots on the footpaths as the men made their way toward the pit. Imagine entering the cage to go underground for the day, not seeing daylight for eight or more hours with only the light of your lamp, swallowing coal and stone dust for hours on end, often up to your waist in water. Most times, the miners would be lying on their sides working in coal seams only 18 inches in height. The sound of the pit buzzer during shifts would strike fear into the women folk expecting the worst. Another fear was if the ambulance man called to the house. This would always mean an accident underground involving a trip to the hospital.

That coal industry and its men served this country well in both wartime and peace time. The cost to them and their families has been enormous. Apart from the large tragedies such as the Stanley Burns Pit, which cost 168 men and boys to lose their lives, and later the Morrison Disaster, which cost 22 lives, many more died in single death accidents. The cost to them and their families was unmeasurable.

Even those who were not killed did not get away with it. Most of the earlier miners probably had either silicosis (coal dust lung infection) or pneumonicosis (stone dust lung infection). I know of one man in recent years who had only been recorded as having 5% silicosis. Just before he died his surgeon wrote off to those concerned that in his opinion, after surgery, this man was most probably 100% infected with the said disease. He died within weeks.

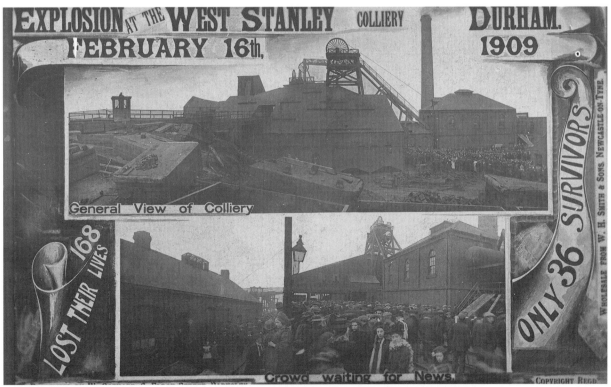

A memorial postcard for the West Stanley Colliery disaster of 1909.

I have talked to many others in a similar situation. It bothers me that there was and is such a discrepancy in the figures. After all, the particular miner mentioned did not work in the pit after his first diagnosis. So I ask, where did it come from? It suggests it was there all the time and he received no payment for the degree of the illness. Poor reward for a life in the pits.

When my dad was in the wrong shift I would get the job of walking down to East Tanfield Pit Offices to get his pay. While there I used to pay his union dues. He later transferred to East Tanfield Drift situated around the Old Causey Road. My Uncle Bob Austin also worked at the drift and he sought permission to take me underground for a look around. After picking up our hats and electric head lamps, we walked down the slope into the drift. With each step we took it got darker and darker and soon all I could see was the area directly in front of me, illuminated by the small head lamp. I found this very uneasy and I was nervous as to what to expect. We finally reached what I would call complete blackness on every side of me. I never dreamed anything could be so dark. I felt the warmth of the air and a smell I can't describe – a sort of damp, humid smell. We stayed there a while, looking where the coal had been removed and at some of the equipment used. I was pleased when we turned around to head back to the surface and daylight. When my dad got to know I'd been down the drift he was not too pleased and said that one member of the family down the pit was too many. During his working life, Dad never lost a shift unless he'd been injured. On one such occasion he was working late, preparing an area for progress, when a 'side wafer' (a large piece of stone) came from above which virtually totally buried him. The men who came to his rescue cleared the loose debris and saw that Dad's feet were the opposite way to his body. They feared his feet had been cut off. However, when they moved this great stone they discovered both feet were broken. He also suffered spine injuries.

Due to the severity of his injuries he lay in the hospital bed for several days, still black with coal dust. His deputy on that shift later told me that they had believed Dad was dead until they removed this huge stone. Dad later returned to work and was employed in the pits until he retired. East Tanfield had closed and he was transferred to Kibblesworth Pit.

For him there was no golden handshake, no gold watch, not even a thank you for a lifetime in a job he never wanted in the first place. I am glad I never worked in the mines but I will always be proud to be the son of that particular coal miner – my dad.

Kibblesworth Colliery. The pit was closed in 1974.

Keep The Home Fires Burning
by Colin Orr

In the same way as New Silksworth's 'Who's Who' has fallen into decay in the last three decades (now no Colliery Manager, nor Engineer, no Police Sergeant, no Durham County Councillor, no Miners' Lodge Chairman, no Co-op Manager, no Senior School Headteacher) so has the 'What's What'!

A significant gap here is the Coal Motor, frequently-seen and as popular a vehicle as any on the streets of the village. A free house and free coal were perquisites (perqs) of the County Durham miner as long ago as Victorian times and possibly even from the days that coal was first mined in the region. Rent and firing, as it used to be known, was a key part of the contract of service. Indeed, should the pit owner be unable to provide a houses for his employee, then an allowance was made in lieu of both the rent and the cost of fuel. In work terms, these dual benefits constituted the miner's family silver and were never negotiable. Any bid to withdraw them would encounter fierce resistance. During the chairmanship of Mr Neddy Pearson at our local Miners' Lodge, the pit would have been loused out (brought out on strike) in seconds if they were under threat.

This was something we quickly learned as boys. If your dad worked at the pit, and most did, then you were all right for coals. A warm living room was guaranteed, even if bedrooms on biting winter nights were as cold as Greenland's icy mountains.

Our council house in The Crescent was different, but it seemed that colliery cottages had been designed with this constant, plentiful supply of coal in mind. This struck me on visits to Uncle Andy and Aunt Jennie (daughters, Ivy, Rose and Lily) in George Street East and to a fire place behind which it appeared possible to throw half a ton of

Miners cottages in Mary Street, New Silksworth, are seen being demolished in the 1970s.

coals. There, when the fire needed building up, a trip to the coalhouse was not needed. Only an arm's-length away on the hearth lay the coal rake and a few forward strokes of this had the flames shooting up the chimney in seconds. Further replenishments could be made without exhausting what lay there. I'm certain when I say that loads were delivered at not less than three, but not more than four, weekly intervals – something like 25 days to be more precise. The ticket had to be put in, as the saying went, and within a few days the coal motor (driven by Mr Jack Walker) was heading in your direction. It would be bad management if your coalhouse was empty and you were borrowing to keep a fire going before the coals were dumped. Occasionally, though, and particularly during a hard winter, the bottom of the coal house might be only inches away from view. By then, for certain, you would be burning what was known as duff. This was not much more than coal dust, a shovelful of which had a dramatic beneficial effect, but only momentarily. It quickly caked the surface and deadened the glow.

The newly-supplied load almost surely contained a lot of roundies (large chunks of coal) and the transformation by burning this was both pleasing and cheering. The fire had a fresh vitality and a sense of contentment settled on the household. The day was made and it didn't seem a bad thing after all to have a dad who worked at the pit, dirty and dangerous though the job was. Reading your Biggles book, or listening to Radio Stagshaw or Radio Droitwich, had an enjoyable added dimension. With the flames licking into those roundies, a retreat was required. To stay too close quickly gave you what was popularly referred to as corned-beef legs, a condition that more readily affected the ladies.

Should a neighbour, or someone in the Store butcher queue, announce that , 'It's rubbish they are leading at present,' then here was bad news for those expecting a

A hearth and kitchen range in a Durham cottage. To the right is a mangle and hand wash tub.

George Street West, New Silksworth, comes under the demolition hammer in the 1970s.

delivery. Rubbish signified coal of inferior quality, perhaps with as much duff as roundies, and, more importantly, a big share of stones. Such loads reflected the nature of the coal currently being mined and little could be done. They had not to be interpreted as a spiteful act by the management should output have fallen away. Stones were easily identified, a lighter colour to start with, heavier too, and the large pieces set aside. Small fragments, however, could make their way on to the fire with noisy and potentially dangerous consequences. Now, the back-away exercise was not due to excessive heat, but in a bid to find shelter.

That Bobby Thompson joke about China figures, notably one of Napoleon, in a miner's cottage lifting their arms to protect themselves from flying pieces of hot stone had everything to do with such a load of coal. It would need no explanation in County Durham. Once a pit mishap had reduced the number of my dad's legs from two to one, to make him a compensation case, the job of housing our coals fell to brother Albert, and me. If that brightly-burning fire initiated by a new delivery was the plus, then getting it into the coalhouse was a minus. Washing day was known as the Devil's Birthday, but this was Old Nick's Christmas Day. To count each shovelful that our juvenile limbs hurled through the hatch was the worst thing to do. Complete demoralisation set in when, on reaching 50, the load looked no smaller. Hours and many aching bones later, just enough energy remained to climb into the bath and then into bed. The thought did not strike me then, but it does now, that coals and me did not mix. Thank goodness, I would be leaving school when the opportunities were such that you had not to follow your dad into the pit.

Mine did, and thousands others too. No fun. Hard work if putting in a load of coals was anything to go by.

The Devil's Birthday
by Colin Orr

It was silly, a waste of breath, indeed, to ask your mother as a new week got under way on a Sunday, when she would be doing the washing. There was only one answer. At New Silksworth, as in every other colliery village throughout County Durham and Northumberland, the Devil's Birthday was Monday. And this was a devil who had 52 birthdays a year. 'I only wash once a fortnight,' would never be a comment in the Store butcher queue on a Friday morning. It seemed that miners' wives were ordained to spend Mondays in front of the poss tub and just about every other housewife as well. I was born on an August Monday afternoon and I don't doubt that my man had spent a few hours sossing the dirty clothes before her working day was interrupted. One form of labour was followed by another. Which was worse?

Washing day, and I'm thinking in particular of those in the mid and late 1930s, was jolly hard work. Whether the clothes were pounded in an old fashioned poss tub, which ours was, wooden, heavy, bulky, or in the later dolly tub, metal, light, portable, a Monday's washing knocked the stuffing out of the womenfolk of that day. In homes filled with umpteen bairns, not an altogether uncommon situation, it must have seemed never-ending. Bear in mind, please, that the water supply to a colliery house, Tunstall Terrace, Castlereagh Street, Londonderry Street, and the like, was a single tap at the bottom of the backyard. There was no electricity. In some of those backyards, there might be a wooden shed, the wash house, which was the centre of washing-day operations. On a fine day, the poss tub, depending on the type, would be rolled or carried to the centre of the yard. The gain here was that it took part of washing day out of the living quarters. There was much to be gained here. You could read your comic indoors in comfort.

For us, though, on the Newport Estate, Silksworth, and everyone else in a Council House of that era, the Devil's Birthday was celebrated indoors. There were no backyards, but we were three goals in front by having both hot and cold water on tap inside the house. Another plus was the set-pot built into the wall next to the coal fire. Mind you, had there been space outside, it would have been impossible to get the tub outside. Its girth was such that it could not be carried and I'm sure the house was built around it! From one Monday to another, it was stored in the cupboard underneath the stairs, leaving just enough room for my mam to shelter there during thunderstorms. Later, in night air-raids, it provided refuge for my dad. Getting to the Anderson shelter at the bottom of the garden on a wooden crutch in the dark was no easy job. If the coal fire had not gone out, it was warmer, too.

Younger mams, and consequently smaller families,

G. Dawson using a poss and mangle at New Lambton in the 1930s.

might take washing day in their stride to claim that they had everything out of the way by tea-time, but that would hardly be the end of the story. Stage one was over. For the less sprightly, and my mother was one, coming up to 37 when I was born, it could be Thursday afternoon when washing day ultimately came to a close. Several piles of ironing had to be dealt with by a couple of flat irons, warmed on a tiny gas ring. Nor had we one of those fancy contraptions that you raised by a pulley to the ceiling to help the clothes dry. Three hooks at different points in the picture rail and a clothes line to form a triangle was a less-sophisticated drying arrangement. Dodging the wet garments was a skill in itself. Without it, the sides of your face were never dry. Cold winter nights made the experience more unpleasant.

The poss tub, of course, didn't work without the poss stick and ours must have been one of the heaviest in the colliery. It was far from slimline and even one of Curtly Ambrose's physique would not have found it comfortable to manage, let alone my slightly-built mam. The very nature of its function caused it to become heavier as the dirty water soaked into its base, long since distorted by years of pounding. One blow over the head from it would have brought any burglar's career to a sudden end. Much smaller in size and much less in weight, too, was the scrubbing brush, but its capacity to sap the user's energy was equally devastating. Getting rid of the dirt and grease from cuffs and collars tested every neck, shoulder and arm muscle. Waking up on Tuesday morning could be a painful exercise.

It was no surprise then that you found your mam in no mood for telling jokes when you reached home from school on a Monday lunchtime. Tired folk find it hard to be comical. If it was a dull, damp, depressing November day, anything but what your mam was wanting for a washing day, and you had had a bad time with the daily mental arithmetic test, then your cup of woe was overflowing. There would be nothing to raise your spirits in what your mam was about to put down in front of you as a meal, and you knew this, too. Hastily, the top of the table had been dried off, the oil cloth laid, but no pleasant surprises were in store. On a Monday, the only item on the menu was what was popularly known in every mining village as Cald, Warmed Up! Put another way – what had been left from Sunday's lunch and now heated in the oven. Dutifully, but never eagerly, you tucked into it.

The good news at tea-time was that the poss tub was back under the stairs and going to bed, having read that day's issue of the *Adventure*, was brightened by the knowledge that the next Devil's Birthday was as far away as it was possible to be. In Durham Prison, inmates would be retiring for the night, not having put in as hard a shift as your mam had standing at that poss tub. They were on hard-labour sentences too!

Dora and Hannah Blenkinsop doing the washing at Stanhope around 1910. Dora is using the poss tub while Hannah is wringing out.

169

The opening of Tanfield Lea Welfare Park, 16th July 1936.

Welfare Pavilion and Bowling Green, Blackhall Colliery, just after it was opened in the 1930s. At one time miners at Blackhall contributed 2d a week towards the welfare scheme. This provided funds of £975 a year.

Celebrating Nationalisation at Murton, 1st January 1947.

A Charlaw & Sacriston Coal Company wagon at the Victory Celebrations in 1919. Peace Day in 1919 saw great scenes of remembrance in the colliery villages of Durham for those who had fallen during the First World War.

Growing flowers has always been a popular pitman's pastime. This chrysanthemum show is believed to be in the Annfield Plain area. Note the flowers have been placed in Federation Brown Ale bottles. Second from the right is Billy Lees.

Left: A miner admires his blooms in his green house in Waldridge in 1937.

Workingmen's Club & Institute, Cornsay Colliery. The club or institute was often at the centre of activities in colliery villages. Sadly, many have closed since the decline of mining in the county.

Here are four photographs taken at Chester Moor Colliery which are very informal views of pit life.

James Forster with his sinker's gear on shows Hilda Scott from Suffolk around Chester Moor Colliery. Hilda was on holiday and had never seen a coal mine.

Mr Clark, Freda Elliott, Hilda Scott and Mr Gibbons beside the boilerhouse at Chester Moor. Hilda was staying with Freda on her visit to Durham.

Lads riding bare back at Chester Moor. Third from the left is Norman Forster. The main North Eastern Railway Line signal box is to the left.

Norman Forster, Tom Lawson and George Bland pose on an early motorcycle in Chester Moor pit yard. Note the belt drive to the rear wheel.

Acknowledgements

The authors would like to thank the following who have contributed to this book:

Tom Bainbridge, George Bowerbank, Ray Card, Ian S. Carr, Ann Cheetham (née Crawford), Jenny Clasper, Jim Coates, Lena Cooper, Arthur Curtis, Anne Dixon, Dennis Fisher, Andrew Gavaghan, Winifred M. Gray MBE, Morgan Hardy, Thomas Hardy, David Harker, George Hoare, Joan Holmes, John Humble, Tom Hutchinson, Mike Kirkup, Bill Lees, Olive Linge, Billy McKie, Colin Mountford, Tom Nairn, Colin Orr, Jim & Joan Pace, Morris Pitt, Dorothy A. Rand, Stan Rand, Albert Richardson, Michael Richardson, Mary Robinson, Neil Taylor, Steve Tiplady, Terry Valente and John Woodall.

John Gall, Jim Lawson, Julian Harrop and all the staff at Beamish – North Of England Open Air Museum

Brian Thornton, Records Officer, The Coal Authority
Durham City Library
Sunderland Echo
Sunderland Library
University Of Durham Library

The articles 'A State Of The Art Pit' and 'A Day To Remember' were written by Ray Card.

Neil Taylor's article 'The Mighty Leek' was originally published in *People & Places Of Old County Durham*
Jack Hair's articles 'Son Of A Coal Miner' and 'Big Meeting Day' were originally published in *Looking Back At Stanley*
Peter Gibson's article 'Wearmouth At War' was first published by the *Sunderland Echo*

Bowburn Colliery not long after its opening in 1908. The steam crane in the centre, with the vertical boiler, was used for shunting as well as lifting as the pit did not have a traditional 'tankie'.

Felling Colliery, around 1910. It was served by sidings from the Gateshead to South Shields line, west of Felling Station. The colliery was closed in 1931.

Bibliography

Frank Atkinson, *Life And Traditions In Northumberland and Durham*, 1977
Frank Atkinson, *The Great Northern Coalfield 1700-1900*, 1966
George L. Atkinson, *The Miners' Heritage*, 1997
Tom Bainbridge, *The Boldons*, 1998
Geoffrey Berriman, *Houghton-le-Spring*, 2000
Alan Brett, *Vaux Wearside League Centenary*, 1992
Norman Emery, *The Coalminers Of Durham*, 1992
Norman Emery, *Banners Of The Durham Coalfield*, 1998
T.H. Hair, *A Series Of Views Of The Collieries In The Counties Of Northumberland And Durham*, 1844
Tom Hutchinson, *The Gaunless Valley*, 2001
Mike Kirkup, *Eyewitness: The Great Northern Coalfield*, 1999
John Kitching, *Brandon And District*, 2000
Jack Lawson, *A Man's Life*, 1944
Stuart Miller & George Nairn, *Around Washington*, 1998
Colin Mountford & L.G. Charlton, *Industrial Locomotives of Durham*, 1977
William A. Moyles, *Mostly Mining*, 1969
J.N. Pace & Andrew Clark, *Ryhope And Silksworth*, 1997
George Parkinson, *True Stories Of Durham Pit-Life*, 1912
Douglas Pocock, *A Mining World – The Story of Bear Park*, 1985
Gordon Stridiron, *A History of Wardley, Its Colliery and People*
Peter A. White, *Portrait Of County Durham*, 1967
Trevor Williamson, *Images Of Seaham*, 1999

The Bather's Handbook, National Coal Board, 1956
A Century Of Care, Durham Aged Miners' Homes Association, 1998
Colliery Guardian, Guide To The Coalfields, 1959
Opening Of New Hall And Offices, Durham Miners' Association, 1915
The Usher Magazine

THE MINERS SMILE AT LAST.

We are unsure where this photograph was taken and why it is captioned 'The Miners Smile At Last'. However, it is the perfect image to end this People's History of Durham Coal. Here we have a smiling group of marras. Times were often hard in the pits but the comradeship of your fellow worker was something that you would not forget. This book is dedicated to all those who worked in the collieries of a county built on coal.

The People's History

To receive a catalogue of our latest titles send a large SAE to:

The People's History
Suite 1
Byron House
Seaham Grange Business Park
Seaham
County Durham
SR7 0PY